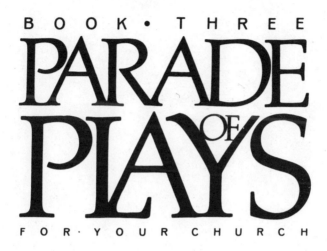

BOOK · THREE

PARADE OF PLAYS

FOR · YOUR · CHURCH

David C. Cook Publishing Co.
© 1985 Elgin, Illinois—Weston, Ontario

PARADE OF PLAYS 3
For Your Church

Second Printing, March 1989

© 1985 David C. Cook Publishing Co., Elgin, IL 60120. Cable
address: DCCOOK. Printed in U.S.A. All rights reserved.
Plays in this book may be reproduced for use in the church
without the written permission of the publisher.
Editors: Lucy F. Townsend, Eric Potter, and Kent Lindberg
Cover and text design: Barbara Sheperd Tillman
ISBN: 0-89191-281-9

Preface

When I was in second grade, I acted in my first school play. The night of the performance my mother dressed me in a starched red dress with a white apron she had made just for the occasion. Then she handed me a plate of heart-shaped cookies with red icing. The play was a dramatization of Mother Goose's familiar rhymes. I said eight lines.

I loved it all—my costume, my lines, my cookies, and most of all the excitement of being onstage. I don't remember much about second grade, but I'll never forget that play.

I've seen the same excitement I felt in second grade on the faces of hundreds of costumed kids parading across stage or sanctuary platform. Ah, the power of a play!

Drama is one of the best ways to help people capture the reality of the Christian life. Like Moses, your players can miraculously part the Red Sea. Like Deborah, they can save their people, the chosen of God. And like Peter they can weep over their betrayal of their best friend and Lord. Through such dramatic acts, actors and audience will experience vicariously what it means to "walk by faith and not by sight."

This book is a collection of plays written for you—the Christian leader who may never have tried drama before. **Parade of Plays 1, 2,** and **3** contain skits, choral readings, puppet shows, mimes, musicals, and radio dramas which can be used in a variety of church settings. Some are especially for young children. Others can be acted by teens and adults. Also included are helpful suggestions from amateur directors on staging, costumes, cast, etc.

The key to dramatic success is simplicity. Begin with a simple choral reading and then move on to more elaborate productions. Skim through the book looking for plays that sound interesting. Then stop and dig more deeply. Don't forget to read carefully the staging and costuming suggestions. May God bless you with much joy as you act out His story!

Lucy Townsend, Ph.D.

Preface

Table of Contents

CHRISTMAS AROUND THE WORLD

A Christmas Program

Play Script & Music
by Charlene Hiebert

This program shows how Christians around the world express the personality of their cultures in the celebration of Christ's birth. The program can be used with preschool and elementary children.

Cast:

The cast will consist of two main areas: choir and speaking parts. However, the program can be done without a choir. Assign the countries to various classes. These classes will be responsible for singing the song for their country. For example: First grade—Germany; Second grade—Italy. Or you might combine classes. Kindergarten and preschool children could participate in the choir. Most of the speaking parts are best suited for primary-juniors. Some of the shorter parts could be given to primaries.

Music:

Most of the songs include verses written in other languages. Have the children concentrate on learning the songs in English first. If time allows, go back and learn them in the other languages.

Props:

Most of the props are easily available or can be made. You will need:
- large decorated Christmas tree
- small table covered with a pretty Christmas cloth
- rocking cradle
- sock filled with corn
- two baby dolls wrapped in swaddling clothes

- script stand and stools for the narrators
- script stand for speaking parts—these can be choir music stands
- apple with a ribbon tree hanger tied on it
- Advent wreath—this can be made using a Styrofoam ring, evergreen branches, and four red candles. Cut four holes in the ring slightly smaller than the base of the candles. Pin short pieces of greenery around the ring. Set candles into the holes.
- small tray with a loaf of bread and a pitcher of milk on it
- manger
- posada candles—these can be made using flashlights, long cardboard tubes, colored cellophane, wire, foil gift wrap, and ribbon. Make three seven-inch cuts equal distance from one another in one end of the cardboard tube. Set the flashlight in the end with the cuts and tape it in place. Position the switch so that the flashlight can be turned on and off. Tape loops of wire around the flashlight to make a cage at the end of the candle. Put a large piece of colored cellophane over the cage and gather it at the base. Tie a ribbon around the cellophane to hold it in place. Wrap the rest of the tube in foil.

Sound and Lighting:

If possible, provide a microphone for the narrators and the children with speaking parts.

The lights in the sanctuary should be on until the living manger scene is formed and the Italian speaking parts are finished. Then, if possible, have only stage lights on. This will focus attention on the manger scene and make the entrance of the posada procession more exciting.

The sanctuary lights can come back on for the closing carol if you feel the congregation will need to use songbooks. Or, the carol could be sung by candlelight. When the children set the candles in the window during the Irish presentation, have a child with a lighted taper light each one.

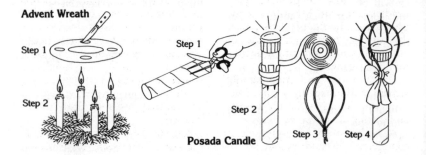

Advent Wreath
Step 1
Step 2

Step 1
Step 2
Posada Candle
Step 3
Step 4

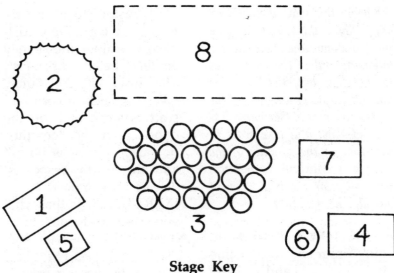

Stage Key

1. Narrators
2. Christmas tree
3. Classes of children for each scene
4. Table
5. Rocking cradle
6. Microphone for speaking parts
7. Manger
8. Choir (optional)

Staging:

As the program begins, the children, except for those in the Irish and Mexican presentations, enter from the back of the church and walk to their seats or positions on stage. The Irish children carrying candles, and the Mexican posada procession should be seated near the back of the church or wait to enter the sanctuary until it is time for their scene.

The narrators and choir should remain on the stage throughout the program, standing for their parts and sitting in between times.

As each country's presentation is completed, the children may return to their seats or join the choir.

Costumes:

The children with speaking parts should dress after the fashion of the country they represent. The children's basic clothing items can be changed to seem more ethnic. Encyclopedias sometimes describe the clothing worn by people of various nations. Such descriptions can provide helpful costume ideas. Of course, picture books about the various countries are the best source for ideas.

Allow choir members to wear any native costume they would like.

Nativity costumes can be made by using bathrobes, choir robes, and shawls.

(To begin this play, the children sing "Joy to the World" as they process down the aisle in the following order: the choir goes to the choir loft; the narrators take their places on stage; the representatives of Germany, Italy, and Australia take seats in the front of the sanctuary; the Irish and Mexican representatives sit near the back or wait outside the sanctuary.)

NARRATOR 1: Welcome to our program. My name is _____ and my very good friend, here, is _____ . We will be your guides this evening as we look at how Christmas is celebrated around the world.

NARRATOR 1 *(noticing the sock held in Narrator 2's hand)*: What's the sock for? Didn't you have enough time to finish dressing?

NARRATOR 2: I've got my socks on! This sock isn't for wearing anyway. It's a Bulgarian sock.

NARRATOR 1: A Bulgarian sock? What's a Bulgarian sock?

NARRATOR 2: In Bulgaria it's a custom to fill a sock with dried corn. On Christmas morning the family gathers before breakfast. The head of the family takes the sock of corn and scatters some of it on the doorstep. As he does this, he says, "Christ is born," and the family responds, "He is born indeed."

NARRATOR 1: Is that what you want us to do?

NARRATOR 2 *(shakes head "yes" and scatters a handful of corn on the floor)*: Christ is born!

NARRATOR 1 and CONGREGATION: He is born indeed!

NARRATOR 1: That was nice, but why did you throw the corn?

NARRATOR 2: It's something the people did before the missionaries brought Christianity to their land. They thought that it would bring them good crops and health. When they became Christians, they mixed some of their old customs with their new beliefs.

NARRATOR 1: That's the same thing that happened

in many countries. Before missionaries brought Christianity to the people of Northern Europe, they worshiped evergreen trees. They thought the trees had special powers because they stayed green during the cold winter weather. When they became Christians, they used the evergreens as symbols of everlasting life. *(Choir stands to sing while German children walk to the front.)*

CHOIR: "O Christmas Tree"

(German children may join in singing as they enter. They bring with them the Advent wreath and an apple.)

_____ *(First German child)*: Guten Abend. (GOO-ten Ah-bent) We would like to tell you about Christmas in Germany. The people of Germany have known about Christianity for more than 1,000 years.

_____ *(Second German child)*: We would like to tell you how the evergreen tree became a Christmas tree. In the Middle Ages, Christians celebrated Adam and Eve Day on December 24. Plays were put on to show how sin first entered the world. One of the favorite props used in these plays was a Paradise Tree. It was usually an evergreen tree with apples tied on its branches. Later, when they stopped having the plays, the people of Germany began putting the trees up in their homes on Christmas Eve as decorations. *(Step back.)*

(Third German child comes forward holding the apple.)

_____ *(hold up the apple)*: This was the first Christmas tree decoration. Over the years, it was joined by candles and Communion bread. Today, colored balls usually replace the apples and electric lights replace the candles.

(Hang the apple on the Christmas tree.)

(The Advent wreath children come to the microphone.)

_____ *(hold the wreath up)*: In German homes, the Christmas tree is one of the

11

last decorations to be put up, but the Advent wreath is one of the first. Beginning with the fourth Sunday before Christmas, the family gathers around it once a week to light certain candles, read Scripture passages, sing, and pray. The candles symbolize the coming of Jesus, the Light of the World. As the candles are lit, they are a reminder of the true meaning of Christmas.

_____ : On the second Sunday of Advent, both the Bethlehem and Prophet candles are lit. The Bethlehem candle is a reminder that God keeps His promises. He sent the Messiah and He was of David's line, just as the prophets foretold.

_____ : Three candles are lit on the third Sunday of Advent. The new candle is called the Shepherd's candle. It is a reminder that even though the shepherds were afraid, they listened, believed, and obeyed the angel's message.

_____ : On the last Sunday of Advent, all four candles are lit. The fourth candle is called the Angel candle. It is a reminder that the angels brought the Good News that the Light of the World had come.

(Set the wreath on the table.)

_____ : Before we leave we would like to wish you a Merry Christmas in German.

ALL: Fröliche Weinachten! (FREE-li-kah VYE-nahkten) *(Exit.)*

NARRATOR 2: That was all very interesting.

NARRATOR 1: Ireland is our next country.

CHOIR *(stand to sing)*: "Here We Come A-Caroling"

(Irish children place candles in each of the church windows before coming on stage. They can join the choir in singing as they work. The first child to speak goes directly on stage carrying a tray with bread and milk on it.)

_____ : On Christmas Eve, an Irish family places a candle in each of their windows. These candles are left burning throughout the night. They serve as an invitation to any travelers who, like Mary and Joseph, might find themselves in need of food or shelter. When the family goes to bed, they leave the doors unlocked and set bread and milk out on a table, so that their hospitality is thus extended throughout the night.

_____ : The Irish people seldom decorate their homes with Christmas trees. They prefer a simple Nativity scene and the window candles. Before we leave we would like to wish you a Merry Christmas in Gaelic.

ALL: Nodlaig mhaith chugnat! (NOHD-lye mithe HIN-uh) *(Exit.)*

NARRATOR 2: Our third country is Italy. Italy's Christian roots go all the way back to Bible times. The Italian people have started many of the Christmas customs that other countries now follow. Some of these are singing carols and ringing church bells.

CHOIR *(have it stand to sing):* "Sleep, O Sleep, My Lovely Child"

(Italian children enter. The children with speaking parts come to the microphone. The others form a living manger scene. The manger is empty at this point.)

_____ : The manger scene has always been an important part of Italy's Christmas celebration. They had the first live manger scene written about in history.

_____ : Today at Christmas, every church, home, and business has a carved manger scene on display.

(The lighting should focus on the living manger scene.)

NARRATOR 1: Thank you. Would you please wish us Merry Christmas in Italian before you leave?

CHILDREN WITH SPEAKING PARTS: Buone Fests Natalizie! (BOHN-ay FEST-ay nah-tah-LEETS-ey-ay)

(Speakers exit; manger scene remains onstage.)

NARRATOR 1: The Italians have shared their love of manger scenes with the people of many other lands.

NARRATOR 2: Yes, that's right, and our next country is one of them. Let's welcome the representatives of Mexico. *(The three children with speaking parts enter.)*

_____ : Christmas in Mexico is a colorful mixture of parties and religious services.

_____ : The posadas (po-SAH-duhz) are reenactments of Mary and Joseph's search for shelter. For nine nights, from December 16 through December 24, friends and relatives carry the figures of Mary and Joseph through the streets. As they travel by the light of the paper lanterns they carry, they sing songs asking for shelter for the holy couple. Only the home chosen for that evening will allow them entrance. Once inside the home, they go from room to room where there are people playing the part of innkeepers. They are turned away by each one until they come to the room where the manger scene has been set up. The figures of Mary and Joseph are put in place and prayers are said. Then everyone goes outside to the patio for a party where they'll have food, fireworks, and a piñata.

_____ : The last posada on Christmas Eve is the biggest celebration. The figure of the Christ Child is carried through streets lined with paper lanterns to light His way.

(Mexican procession enters from the back of sanctuary.)

CHOIR AND MEXICAN CHILDREN: "Pray Give Us Lodging"

(The children place the figure of the Christ Child in the manger. The Mexican children stand across the front of the church but do not go onstage.)

NARRATOR 1: We have talked about a lot of different customs!

NARRATOR 2: Yes, and we still have one country to go.

NARRATOR 1: What country is that?

NARRATOR 2: It's Australia. Since Australia's seasons are the opposite of the northern hemisphere's, its Christmas comes during the summertime. Here come the Australian representatives to tell us how they celebrate Christmas.

_____ : A popular Australian Christmas Day activity is to picnic at the beach.

_____ : Australia's most famous custom is the radio program called "Carols by Candlelight." In 1937 a radio announcer, named Norman Banks, saw a lonely old woman listening to carols on the radio. He decided to invite his listening public to join him on the banks of a Melbourne river for a carol sing by candlelight. It was so well attended that he made it a regular Christmas event. Today more than 250,000 people gather in the parks of Australia on Christmas Eve to sing songs of praise. Their voices are sent by radio waves into the homes of the sick and elderly.

NARRATOR 1: Let's join this custom. Will you all stand and join us in singing "Hark! the Herald Angels Sing."

(When the song is finished Narrator 2 takes the sock and sprinkles more corn.)

NARRATOR 2: Yes, Christ is born! He is born indeed!

(Prayer by minister.)

15

O Christmas Tree

Old German Traditional

O Christmas Tree **German**

O Tannenbaum, O Tannenbaum,
Wie treu sind deine Blatter.
Du grunst nicht nur zur Sommerzeit,
Nein, auch im Winter, wenn es schneit.
O Tannenbaum, O Tannenbaum,
Wie treu sind deine Blatter.

Here We Come A-Caroling

Traditional English

1. Here we come a car - o - ling, A - mong the leaves so green;
2. God bless the mas - ter of this house, and bless the mis - trees, too, And

Here we come a wan - d'ring, So fair to be seen.
all the lit - tle chil - dren, That round the ta - ble go.

Love and joy come to you, And a mer - ry Christ-mas, too; And God bless you and send you a hap - py New Year, And God send you a hap - py New Year.

Sleep, O Sleep, My Lovely Child

Italian

Dormi, dormi, o bel bambin,
Re divin, Re divin.
Fa la nanna, o fantolino,
Re divin, Re divin.
Fa la nanna, o fantolino.

Sleep, O Sleep, My Lovely Child

Traditional Italian

Pray Give Us Lodging

Traditional Mexican Carol

♩=138

San Jose: 1. En___ NOHM-bray___ dell see-EL - oh. Ohs-pee-doh___
Joseph: 1. Pray give us lodg-ing, dear sir, in the name of Heav'n! All day since morn-ing
Host: 2. You can-not stop here, I won't make my house an inn; I do not trust you.
Joseph: 3. Please show us pit-y! Your heart can-not be this hard! Look at poor Mar-y,
Host: 4. You try my pa-tience! I'm tired and must get some rest; I've told you nice-ly,
Joseph: 5. Sir, I must tell you, my wife is___ the___ one, Chos-en by God to
Host: 6. Jo-seph, dear Jo-seph! O how could I be so blind? Not to know you and

poh - SAII - - dah Poo-AYS no PWAY-day ahn - DAR___
to tra-vel___ we've___ giv'n, Ma-ry, my wife, is ex-pect-ing a
Your sto-ry___ is___ thin. You two might rob me and then___ run a-
so worn and so___ tired! We are most poor, but I'll pay___ what I
de-liv-er___ His___ Son. Je-sus is com-ing to earth___ on this
the Vir-gin___ so___ fine! En-ter, blest pil-grims, my house___ is your

Mee___ es-POH-sah ah-MAH - - dah.
child; She must have shel-ter to-night. Let___ us___ in, let___ us___ in!
way; Find some-where else you can stay. Go___ a - way! go___ a - way!
can; God will re-ward you, good man! Let___ us___ in, let___ us___ in!
me; I'll fix you, I guar-an-tee! Go___ a - way! go___ a - way!
eve; O God, please make him be-lieve! Let___ us___ in, let___ us___ in!
own; Praise be to God on His throne! Please___come___ in, please___come___ in!

Pray Give Us Lodging Spanish

En nombre del cielo,
Os pido posada
Pues no puede andar
Mi esposa amada.

Let All God's Creatures Rejoice!

A Christmas Program
by Lucy F. Townsend

This Christmas program involves preschool and elementary children in a joyful celebration of Jesus' birth.
Dressed as bells, angels, stars, and animals, young children recite poetry and sing favorite Christmas songs. Older children play musical instruments, act as ushers, and perform in a tableau.

A week before Jesus' death, He said that if people hadn't praised Him as the King of the Jews, the stones in the street would have shouted His praise. This program dramatizes what the rest of God's creation might do if people refused to celebrate the birth of the long-awaited Messiah.

Cast:
Bells (2- to 3-year-olds)
Angels (4- to 5-year-olds)
All God's Creatures (elementary children; "creatures" might be fish, frogs, birds, camels, lions, insects, trees, stars, etc.)

Mary
Joseph
Donkey
Shepherds
Wise Men
Narrators
Choirs
Ushers

Costumes:
These can be simple or elaborate, depending on your resources. Bells might be cut from cardboard and decorated with silver spray paint. Attach bells with elastic neck straps to the children. You might also add red ribbons at children's necks. Actors dressed like animals can

attach the names of the animals to the front of their shirts. Cut out construction paper or fabric spots and pin these to the children's clothing. If more elaborate costumes are worn, be sure to keep children's faces uncovered. Mary, Joseph, shepherds, and Wise Men can wear typical Bible-time costumes—bathrobes, shawls, and sandals. Ushers might also dress up like reptiles, insects, fish, trees, the moon, etc.

Advance Preparations:

Write a letter to parents and Sunday school teachers. Explain your goals for the program as well as dates and times of rehearsals and the Christmas performance. You might also ask a class of older children to design the cover for the bulletin insert. They might draw a picture of various animals praising God. On the back, duplicate names of everyone with a part in the program. Ask all children to bring a gift-wrapped Christmas present to present to Jesus. These might be canned goods, clothing for needy people, items for the church or missionaries, etc. Encourage the children to think and pray about what they might bring. Gifts should be put on the floor beside each child's seat until the end of the program.

Tableau: Set up a manger scene to one side of the platform. You will need actors to play Mary and Joseph and their donkey, but do not include any other people. Tableau actors do not have to say lines or sing. Throughout the program, they will simply stay in place. Two

or more children could play shepherds.

Ask an older child/teen to accompany singers on the piano, flute, violin, or other musical instrument. Special numbers might be played before the program begins.

BELLS *(2- to 3-year-olds play this part. Each child wears a large cardboard bell over his or her clothing. Some tie bells on their shoes. Others carry different-sized bells. If you have a microphone, have children say their lines into it.):*

We are shiny Christmas bells,
Can you hear us ring?
Christmas is a happy time,
So we laugh and sing.

(Children jingle their bells.)

SONG *(sing to the tune of "Jingle Bells"):*

Jingle bells, jingle bells,
Christ is born today,
Tell the world the Savior's come,
He's lying in the hay,

Jingle bells, jingle bells,
Jingle all the way,
Won't you help us celebrate
The Savior's special day!

(Piano or other instrument plays third verse. Children jingle bells but do not sing. They leave stage jangling bells.)

NARRATOR 1: Christmas is a very special time of year when everyone celebrates. The tiniest children jingle their little Christmas bells. Church choirs sing praises to God. And like the Wise Men, we all share our treasures. Let's retell the Christmas story to see just why everyone is so happy.

NARRATOR 2: *(Mary, Joseph, and donkey proceed up church aisle to the manger scene and take their places.)* In those days Caesar Augustus issued a decree that a census should be taken of the entire Roman world. And everyone went to his own town to register. So Joseph also went up from the town of Nazareth in Galilee to Judea, to Bethlehem the town of David, because he belonged to the house and line of David. He went there to register with Mary, who was pledged to be married to him and was with child.

NARRATOR 3: While they were there, the time came for the baby to be born, and she gave birth to her firstborn, a son. She wrapped him in cloths and placed him in a manger, because there was no room for them in the inn. *(Mary should wrap a doll in a blanket and lay it in the manger.)*

NARRATOR 4: *(Shepherds and sheep settle downstage right. They should stay in this spot throughout the program.)* And there were shepherds living out in the fields nearby, keeping watch over their flocks at night. *(Pause while sheep pretend to eat grass. One sheep makes baaing sound. The shepherds stand watch, yawning occasionally. Organist or other instrumentalist plays first verse of "While Shepherds Watched Their Flocks.")* An angel of the Lord appeared to them, and the glory of the Lord shone around them, and they were terrified.

ANGELS *(4- to 5-year-olds play these parts. Each child wears a white tunic or choir*

robe. Wings might be cut from cardboard and spray painted with silver. Border them with silver garlands. Angels go onstage, preferably a bit above shepherds. They should say the following poem with motions):
Swiftly, swiftly, spread the news, *(hands cupped at mouth)*
Something's happened to the Jews, *(arms outstretched)*
God has sent His only Son, *(point upward)*
Praise Him! He's the Holy One! *(hands outstretched, palms up)*
You can go and kneel nearby, *(kneel down, point to audience)*
Whisper, or he'll wake and cry, *(finger up to lips)*
Put your treasures at his feet, *(pretend to put down treasures)*
Praise Him! Praise Him! We repeat. *(arms outstretched)*
(Angels stand and repeat first verse.)
Song: "Away in the Manger"
NARRATOR 2: Then the angels left the shepherds and went back to heaven. *(Pause while angels leave stage.)* The shepherds said, "Let's go to Bethlehem . . ." *(Shepherds yawn and pretend to go to sleep.)* Wait a minute. *(louder)* The shepherds said, "Let's go to Bethlehem . . . *(pause)* Well, folks, the shepherds have gone to sleep! I wonder why they aren't doing anything about the news from heaven? Well, on with our story . . .

(Organist or other instrumentalists plays first verse of "We Three Kings." Several Wise Men go onstage and point up as if they were looking at something unusual in the sky. They pretend to talk among themselves about the star.)

NARRATOR 3: After Jesus was born in Bethlehem in Judea, during the time of King Herod, some Wise Men saw the star in the East. They were sure the star must signify the birth of a special king, so they traveled to Jerusalem to worship the child. *(Wise Men pretend to take out food and eat. They talk among themselves. Then they wave*

25

good-bye and go offstage.)
Wait a minute! The Wise Men were supposed to travel to Jerusalem. What's wrong with those guys?
NARRATOR 2: Well, something's wrong, folks. The people in the Christmas story simply aren't cooperating. They've heard the angels. They've seen the star, and they don't seem to be the least bit excited. They are pretending that nothing special has happened at all. *(Elementary children dressed up as animals, plants, planets, stars, etc., come onstage.)* Hey, what are all you creatures doing up here? This is a Christmas program!

(For this poem, assign some lines to the specific "creatures." Have all creatures say "Praise God," clap their hands, and stomp their feet. One child might hold a bell which is rung in Stanza 4.

A baby is born tonight;
Praise God!
The angels are filled with delight,
Praise God!

For the King of Creation
Is bringing salvation,
The camels are kneeling
God's creatures are feeling
Great joy for the Savior,
Praise God!
The sheep spread the wonderful news!
(clap, clap)
A King has been born to the Jews!
(clap, clap)
The bullfrogs are singing,
The bees have stopped stinging,
In honor of Jesus
(clap, clap)
The camels and donkeys bow down,
(stomp, stomp)
This boy should be wearing a crown,
(stomp, stomp)
The lions are roaring,
The sea gulls are soaring,
They sing to the Savior,
(stomp, stomp)
The stars join the heavenly song.
(ping! ping!)
The sun and the moon hum along.
(ping! ping!)
A new star is blazing
It's truly amazing,

This joy for the Savior,
Come celebrate Jesus' birth,
too. *(one voice)*
Praise God!
It's really no fun without
you. *(several voices)*
Praise God!
We're clapping and laughing, *(more voices)*
Jumping and prancing.
The mountains are ringing,
The whole world is singing,
(all voices)
In joy for the Savior,
Praise God!
NARRATOR 1: This is truly
amazing! The animals and
plants and mountains and
lakes and rivers are **all**
praising God! Why, it's
unbelievable!

(Animals go to their seats, pick up Christmas gifts and take them onstage to the Nativity scene.)

What's going on here? Now
they are taking gifts to the
Christ Child. This is incredible! *(After all gifts are placed onstage, animals stand together onstage.)*
Song: "All Creatures of Our
God and King"

(Creatures repeat the last verse of the poem above, inviting the congregation to join them in celebrating the birthday of the King. Then the shepherds and Wise Men take their gifts and place them at the manger, too. They kneel there.)

NARRATOR 1: Well, folks,
the people in this Christmas program have finally
decided to praise God for
His Son, Jesus. Let's join
them in praising God, too.
Sing together "Joy to the
World.")

(Congregation and actors sing the final Christmas hymn.)

The Fourth Shepherd

Christmas Play for Teens
by Barbara Jurgensen

This Christmas play, written for teens, shows how God can use loving Christians to soften even the hardest hearts.

Cast:
Narrator
Hazaiah—(huh-ZAY-uh) a teenager
Jehu—(JEE-hew) another teenager, his brother
Bedad—(BE-dad) a cynic
Obed—(O-bed) a believer, an old man
Herald angel
Other angels
First villager
Second villager
Third villager
Fourth villager

Sound effects: wolf howling, wind, fire

ACT I

NARRATOR: It is night on a hillside near Bethlehem nearly twenty centuries ago. The night is dark. From somewhere not too far away, a wolf sets up a lonely howl. A group of shepherds are sitting on the dry grass of the hillside, watching their sheep. Two of the shepherds are teenagers, taking the place of their father.

HAZAIAH *(deep in thought)*: I worry about Dad. He looked worse tonight.

JEHU *(slowly)*: He didn't look good. He was breathing so fitfully that I was afraid he wouldn't find his next breath.

HAZAIAH: All the doctors and medicines haven't been able to help.

JEHU: If there just was something we could do for him, Hazaiah!

HAZAIAH: We've prayed for him. Since the day he got sick, we've prayed that God would make him well. And he's prayed too.

JEHU: We've all prayed . . .

BEDAD *(scoffing)*: You've prayed! A lot of good that does! You pray for your father and he only gets worse! When my son was sick, none of us prayed for him, and he got better!

OBED *(kindly, but trying to teach Bedad something)*: The father of these boys is sick, Bedad. Is this a time to tell them not to pray?

BEDAD *(cynically)*: No time is a time to pray as far as I'm concerned, Obed.

OBED: You're a bitter man.

BEDAD *(matter-of-factly)*: No, not bitter . . . just realistic. A person has to be realistic. This world is full of troubles and I don't think that prayer has ever helped a single one of them.

OBED: You don't believe in God?

BEDAD: I don't believe in anything but what I can see.

OBED: I pity you. *(He thinks a few moments.)* There come times in all of our lives when we realize we need God.

BEDAD: I am not a young man, but I have yet to see the day when I need God.

OBED: The day may come.

BEDAD *(laughs scornfully)*: I hope I don't live long enough to see that day! This world is nothing but trouble, but I have yet to see the trouble that I can't handle. I can make my own way through this rotten world.

OBED: I say that this is not a rotten world. This is God's world, and He made it for a purpose.

BEDAD (*cynically*): Oh, sure!

OBED: And I look for the day when He will send a Savior for mankind as He has promised.

BEDAD (*sneering*): Oh, sure, that'll be the day!

OBED: He will come as a light to this dark world . . . we will find new life in Him.

BEDAD (*wearily*): Look, this world is rotten and dirty. And I'm a practical man. So let's not look for any miracles.

OBED: I look for the miracle every day.

JEHU: At our house we look for the coming of the Savior, too.

HAZAIAH: Father says he hopes to live to see the Savior.

BEDAD (*scoffing*): Well, you may pity me, but I pity you—all three of you. You've put all your hopes in something that will never be.

(*A wolf howls.*)

JEHU (*ignoring Bedad's comment*): Except for that wolf, the night is still—and dark.

HAZAIAH: Father must get tired of sitting out here night after night.

BEDAD (*cynically*): Ha! That's about what life is— darkness and boredom.

(*Suddenly, from the distance, comes the sound of singing: "Joy to the world, the Lord is come. Let earth receive her king . . ." Then a bright light shines in front of the shepherds and an angel appears in it. Bedad seems calm about all this, but the others are afraid. They lean away from the bright light and shield their eyes with their hands. The angel speaks.*)

HERALD ANGEL: Don't be afraid. I have come to bring you good news about a great thing which has happened. Today, in Bethlehem, Christ the Savior was born. And here is how you will find Him: He is wrapped in swaddling clothes and lying in a feedbox for cattle in a barn.

(*Then the herald angel is surrounded by other angels.*)

ANGELS: "Glory to God in the highest, and on earth

peace to men with whom God is pleased!"

(The angels begin singing "Joy to the world," then exit as they reach the last line. When the angels have gone, the three shepherds gradually take their hands away from their faces and go back to their original sitting positions.)

JEHU (with astonishment): That was an angel! Those were all angels!

BEDAD (cynically): Easy there. Don't get excited.

HAZAIAH: Well, they were angels, weren't they? We all saw them! (looks at others for confirmation) Didn't we?

BEDAD (scornfully): I don't know what you thought you saw. I think a bunch of swamp gas gathered together and flared up.

OBED: Well, I know what I saw! And I'm going over to Bethlehem and see for myself. God doesn't send His Son every day! To think that I should live to see His Son come! (He shakes his head in wonder, then looks around at the boys.) You boys want to come with me?

JEHU: I do!

HAZAIAH: Me, too!

BEDAD (drearily): Go ahead. I'll watch the sheep while you three dreamers go off on your wild-goose chase. (Obed and the boys hurry off.) (to himself) Well, they're gone. I suppose this God of theirs has cooked up some new way to ridicule mankind! Wait till they get into that barn. No God is going to have His Son born in a barn. We men can suffer— oh, that's perfectly all right. But you won't catch any God that I've ever heard of inconveniencing Himself in any way. (He settles back to watch the sheep, then, hearing something, puts a hand over his eyes to look off into the distance.) What's this? A band of people coming up the hill? (He tries to make out who they are and then they are with him.)

FIRST VILLAGER: Are Hazaiah and Jehu here?

BEDAD (bewildered by the sudden appearance of all the people): Yes. I mean, no! I mean, they went into town.

SECOND VILLAGER: Into town?

BEDAD: Yes. Into Bethlehem. It seems something was going on there.

(The villagers stand there, not knowing what to say.)

BEDAD *(sensing their uneasiness)*: What is it? What's the matter?

THIRD VILLAGER: It's their father . . . Hazaiah and Jehu's father . . . he died.

BEDAD *(cynically)*: I knew it! Their prayers were all for nothing! That's the way things always go in this world.

FOURTH VILLAGER: But where can we find them?

BEDAD: Find them? I don't know. In a barn somewhere, I guess. Look for a barn where there's a baby—a newborn baby—in the feedbox.

(The villagers look at each other in bewilderment, then back at Bedad. He seems to have nothing more to say, so they leave.)

BEDAD *(cynically)*: The Son of God in a feedbox. A likely story!

ACT II SCENE I

NARRATOR: It is night on the same hillside near Bethlehem, but the time is more than thirty years later. Old Obed, the believer, has been dead for several years. But Bedad, the cynic, is still alive, though he is a very old man. The two teenagers, Jehu and Hazaiah, are now nearly fifty years old.

HAZAIAH: Another dark night! A man wouldn't want to look for a lost sheep on a night like this!

JEHU: And the grass is so dry! We'll be lucky if some nearby shepherd doesn't doze off and let his fire spread across the hillside.

(A wolf gives a lonely howl.)

HAZAIAH: There's that wolf again.

JEHU: It reminds me of that night so long ago when the Savior was born.

HAZAIAH: Obed was with us then. Remember how the three of us went to see the Savior in the barn? How lucky we are to have seen the Savior.

BEDAD (*disgustedly*): Can't you ever forget Him?

JEHU: Forget Him? We have become His followers!

HAZAIAH: After that night, we didn't see any more of Him until just about a year ago. Then we heard that He was over near Bethlehem preaching, so we went to hear Him.

JEHU: He said things that were thrilling! He told us that God loves us so much that He sent His Son to be our Savior! And that a man can be made right with God by believing.

HAZAIAH: He has taught us how to live as sons of God—loving our fellow-man, returning good for evil, forgiving . . .

JEHU: He has taught us to give our lives in service to others!

BEDAD (*cynically*): And you go along with all this, of course?

JEHU: It's the most wonderful thing we've ever heard! It's what we've been waiting for!

BEDAD (*scornfully*): Speak for yourself. I'm only wait-ing for the same thing I've been waiting for for seventy years—to die and be free from this wretched world!

JEHU: You mean you want to die?

BEDAD (*emphatically*): I will welcome death gladly when it comes. No one is more sick of this world than I am.

HAZAIAH: In a way I will welcome death, too, because then I will go to be with the Savior. But for now I would rather go on living. There's so much work here for a believer to do!

BEDAD (*cynically*): Work? What could you ever do that would make any difference in this rotten life?

HAZAIAH: Well, I ask God each day to give me some work to do for Him. I try to serve Him by helping my fellowmen.

BEDAD (*scornfully*): Well, I for one would like to see just one thing that you ever do that makes any kind of difference!

(*A wolf gives another howl.*)

JEHU: The wind is beginning to come up. Listen to the grass rustle. (He picks up some dry grass from the ground and rubs it between his fingers.) If only we could get some rain.

HAZAIAH: Anyone mind if I catch a few winks? No use all of us sitting awake all night.

JEHU: Fine.

BEDAD: Go ahead. (mockingly) We'll wake you up if any of your white-robed friends come.

(Hazaiah pulls his knees up, leans his head against them, and wraps his arms around his legs. He is soon asleep. Bedad yawns a few times, then lies down on his side to rest a bit. His eyes shut. Finally, Jehu puts his hands behind his head and stretches out full length on his back. At first he keeps his head raised up with his hands so that he can look around, but gradually he lets his head down, and soon he, too, falls asleep.)

SOUND EFFECTS: The wind begins to blow fiercely. The wolf gives two long, plaintive howls. Then suddenly there is the crackling noise of fire.
(Bedad sits up, alert. He sniffs quickly. Quickly he shakes the others.)

BEDAD (shouting): Fire! Get up! The hill is on fire!

(Jehu and Hazaiah jump to their feet, looking around.)

BEDAD (He has been counting the sheep, pointing at each of them with his forefinger): One of the lambs is missing! (He looks around.) Gather the sheep together and drive them off to the west over the brook there where they'll be safe and I'll find the lamb.

HAZAIAH: Let me go and look for the lamb! A man your age shouldn't be out wandering in the dark. You could fall!

BEDAD: I've been a shepherd since I was a small boy, and I've never fallen yet. I know this country better than anyone around. Hurry with the sheep. I'll catch up!

(Bedad hurries off into the darkness; Jehu and Hazaiah hurry off in the other direction.)

ACT II SCENE II

NARRATOR: Knowing well where the lambs usually stray to, Bedad has checked all the nearby ravines, but the lamb was not in any of them. Now he is heading for the only other possible place that it can be, a steep, narrow canyon.

Reaching the canyon, he bleats like a lamb and listens for an answer. From below comes a feeble "Baa-a-a-a." Grabbing hold of a low branch of a bush for support, Bedad lowers himself over the edge. Just as he is feeling with his foot for a place to step, the branch he is holding snaps. Twisting and turning, he is catapulted into the canyon. He crashes against a rock at the bottom and crumples up in pain.

BEDAD *(moaning)*: Help me! Someone help me!

(A wolf howls in the distance.)

BEDAD *(in great distress)*: Oh, help me! *(He runs his hand up and down his leg and winces in pain.)* My leg must be broken! *(Now he calls*

more desperately.)* Can't someone hear me?

(The wolf howls again—this time much closer.)

BEDAD: The wolf is coming closer!

(He tries to raise himself up on his good leg and drag himself along, but the effort is too much for him and he falls back trembling. The wolf howls from the cliff directly above him.)

BEDAD *(in alarm)*: The wolf is here already! *(Painfully he turns himself to face it.)* So you've found me, have you? *(He picks up a stone to hurl at the wolf.)* My arm is so numb I can't even throw a stone. Why did I come here anyway? Someone, please help me! *(Keeping an eye on the wolf, he eases himself back down to the ground to rest. As his head reaches the ground he lets out a moan.)*

SOUND EFFECT: *Fire*

(Bedad turns to look.)

BEDAD: The fire! The fire is rushing down the canyon! *(He buries his face in his hands.)* Help me! Oh, God, help me!

ACT III SCENE I

NARRATOR: Jehu and Hazaiah reached the brook. After finding a shallow place, they helped the sheep cross over.

HAZAIAH: I don't like the idea of Bedad out looking for that lost lamb on a dark night like this. An old man like him shouldn't be wandering around in the dark. There are too many holes around here he could fall into.

JEHU: And the wind's shifty. You never know when it'll turn and bring the fire up behind you. Look! *(He points toward the east.)* The fire's heading this way! We're lucky the brook's wide along here!

HAZAIAH: I wonder what's keeping Bedad?

(A wolf howls in the distance.)

JEHU: That old wolf is sure worked up about something tonight!

(There is a low moan in the wind.)

HAZAIAH: You hear that?

JEHU: No. What?

HAZAIAH: It sounded like someone moaning!

JEHU: I don't hear anything.

(There is another low moan—a cross between the wail of the wind and of a human being.)

HAZAIAH: There it is again! I'm worried about Bedad. *(He jumps up.)* You stay here with the sheep. I'm going to look for him!

ACT III SCENE II

NARRATOR: The fire is coming closer down the canyon floor toward Bedad. Above him, the wolf howls plaintively. Bedad tries again to raise himself from the ground, but he can't.

BEDAD *(struggling)*: I have always said that I wanted to die and be rid of this life, but somehow, now that death is so near, I want to live! Oh, God, help me! *(He moans as he tries to move his leg. Then he hears a noise and looks up.)* Another few feet and the fire and the wolf—

HAZAIAH: Bedad! *(He runs to help the old man, then*

37

stops.) There's that wolf. *(Snatching up a stone, he hurls it at the approaching beast.)* Now he's gone. *(He busies himself helping Bedad.)*

BEDAD: You didn't have to come back through the fire for me! You could have stayed in a safe place.

HAZAIAH: I couldn't leave you!

BEDAD *(amazed)*: You didn't have to do it, but you did it! What makes a man risk his life to save someone who didn't think he wanted to live?

HAZAIAH: It all goes back to the Light that came into the world on that dark night years ago. That Light made a difference in my life.

BEDAD *(no longer cynical)*: Yes, there is a difference. Do you think it's too late for me to learn about that Light?

WERE YOU THERE?

An Easter Choral Reading
by Ramona Warren

The following choral reading, written for children and young teens, can be presented Easter morning during the Sunday school or worship hour. Solo parts should be given to those who enjoy reading.
The choral reading requires props. Readers might wear typical Bible-time costumes—bathrobes, shawls, and sandals.

All of the children should stand together in a group. The children with solo parts will step forward to say their parts in front of a microphone (if you have one). When finished, they will step back into the group.

The children in the group should turn to one another as if asking a question when they repeat their phrase: Were you there? See notation on the choral reading for times to use different voice inflections when repeating the phrase.

Solo Parts:
A girl from the group, Peter, Pilate, Roman Soldier, a woman, Mary Magdalene, John, Cleopas, Thomas, Disciples (at least four, but could be as many as eleven)

Choral Reading:
The group should be standing together but moving around as they talk with one another in low voices and whispers as if asking questions and telling about something that has happened.

GIRL FROM THE GROUP: Everyone in the city is talking! We are trying to find out what happened to Jesus. We are asking the people who were there to tell their stories.

CHORUS (*start lower and get louder*): Were you there? Were you there? Were you there?

PETER: I am Peter, one of Jesus' disciples. I was there. I was there in the garden when the soldiers came and took Jesus away. They took Him to be questioned. When someone asked if I was one of His followers, I lied and said I did not even know Him.

(*Peter walks sadly back into the group.*)

CHORUS (*sadly*): Were you there? Were you there? Were you there?

PILATE: I am Pilate, the governor. I was there. I talked with Jesus. I did not think He had done anything wrong. I asked the people what they wanted me to do with Jesus. The people shouted, "Crucify Him!" So I let the people have their way. I did not want any part of it. I let the soldiers take Jesus away.

(*Pilate returns to the group.*)

CHORUS (*still sadly*): Were you there? Were you there? Were you there?

SOLDIER: I am a Roman soldier. I was there. I made fun of Jesus and put a crown of thorns on His head. But as I watched Him on that cross, I knew He wasn't a criminal. He even forgave the people who hurt Him. As He died, I knew that He was truly the Son of God.

CHORUS: Were you there? Were you there? Were you there?

A WOMAN: I am one of the women who went to Jesus' tomb several days after He died on the cross and was buried. I was there. We wanted to put perfume on Jesus' body. When we got to the tomb, it was empty! Jesus was gone! An angel said, "Do not be afraid. Jesus is risen. Go quickly and tell the disciples." We were so happy and excited! We ran to tell them!

CHORUS *(with excitement)*: Were you there? Were you there? Were you there?

MARY: I am Mary. I was there. I was near the tomb crying because I did not know where Jesus was. Then I heard Someone ask, "Why are you crying?" I thought it was the gardener. I asked Him to tell me where Jesus was. Then He said my name and I knew it was Jesus! He really was alive! I was so happy after I talked with Jesus, I ran to tell everyone the Good News.

CHORUS: Were you there? Were you there? Were you there?

JOHN: I am John, Jesus' disciple. I was there. When Mary came to tell us Jesus' tomb was empty, Peter and I ran to look. We saw that Jesus was gone. We knew He was alive.

CHORUS *(happy and excited)*: Were you there? Were you there? Were you there?

CLEOPAS: My name is Cleopas. I'm a follower of Jesus. I was there. I was walking home with a friend. We were talking about Jesus. A Stranger started walking with us. He talked to us about Christ from God's Word. He came to my home. When He blessed the food, we knew He was Jesus!

CHORUS: Were you there? Were you there? Were you there?

THOMAS: My name is Thomas. I was there. The disciples told me Jesus was alive, but I did not believe them. I wanted to touch the nail prints in His hand to know it was really Jesus. Then one day I was with the disciples when Jesus appeared. Jesus told me to touch His hands and side. He said, "Stop doubting and believe." I knew it was really Jesus. I said, "My Lord and my God!" *(Thomas returns to the group.)*

CHORUS: Were you there? Were you there? Were you there?

PETER: I am Peter, Jesus' disciple. I was there. I ran with John to look in the tomb, and later I was with him and the other disciples. Jesus asked me three times if I loved Him. Each time I told Him I did. Jesus told me to follow Him, and to tell others about Him. And that's what I'm going to do.

CHORUS: Were you there? Were you there? Were you there?

DISCIPLES: We are the disciples. We were there.

1st disciple: For the next 40 days Jesus talked to us often about God. We didn't understand everything He told us, but we were so happy He was alive. We worshiped Him.

2nd disciple: Jesus told us, "All authority in heaven and on earth has been given to me. Therefore go and make disciples of all nations, baptizing them in the name of the Father and of the Son and of the Holy Spirit, and teaching them to obey everything I have commanded you. And surely I will be with you always, to the very end of the age."

3rd disciple: We knew what Jesus wanted us to do.

4th disciple: Jesus wanted us to tell everyone the Good News about Him.

5th disciple (*or 1st if only 4*): We had seen everything that had happened. We are Jesus' followers.

6th disciple (*or 2nd if only 4*): Now it was up to us to tell people how much He loves everyone.

All the disciples: We knew that Jesus was really God's Son. We were there!

ALL MY KINGS

A Biblical Radio Drama
by Don Kahle and Chris Bittler

This radio drama, written for older children and teens, covers the history of the United and Divided Kingdoms. It portrays God's Covenant with David and also depicts the Exile, the return to Jerusalem, and the promise of the Messiah given by the prophet Malachi.

"All My Kings" might be an exciting church program if presented as a "live" radio broadcast. You'll need two stand-up microphones: one for the readers and one for sound effects. Kids would need no special costumes, nor would they need to memorize their lines. The drama might be presented as a three-act program. It might also be spread over three consecutive Sundays.

Cast:
See each act and scene.

ACT I, Scene I
Cast:
Narrator
Nathan, the prophet
King David

SOUND EFFECTS Theme Music and Announcer: ("We return once again to 'All My Kings,' the continuing saga of the rulers of God's chosen people. Our exciting story began when God made a covenant with David to establish his kingdom forever. One of his descendants would indeed rule the earth! David was a great guy but some of his heirs weren't so swift. Through all the scandal, war, and intrigue, God remained faithful to His promise. Tune in again as the drama unfolds and God says, 'What am I going to do with ALL MY KINGS?' ")

NARRATOR: Well, when we left last week, King David had just brought back the ark of the Lord to Jerusalem and was discussing his future plans with Nathan, the prophet.

NATHAN: Good job, Dave. You've obeyed God and brought the ark back to Jerusalem where it belongs.

DAVID: I don't know, Nathan. It still doesn't seem right. I mean, we got the ark back here, but am I really honoring God? I'm living in a nice palace and the Lord is camped out in a tent like a Boy Scout. I'd like to build Him a house.

NATHAN: I have a message concerning that.

DAVID: You do? From whom?

NATHAN: The Lord, of course.

DAVID: Oh, right.

NATHAN: The Lord says, "I have followed Israel around and gotten them out of a thousand messes. Whether they were trapped in Egypt, starving in the Sinai, or lost in the wilderness, I pulled them through. I needed no house then, and I need no house now. Come on, Dave, I could prop My feet up on the earth if I felt like it. I could never be stuffed into a little box of a house. Nevertheless, I appreciate the thought. I know you wish only to honor Me. To reward you for that, I will establish your kingdom forever through your family. Through your son, a temple will be built where My chosen people, Israel, will be able to meet with Me."

DAVID: Who am I, and who is my family that God should do this for me? Out of all the nations of the world He chooses puny Israel to live with! There is no one like Him! I heard it with my own ears. Little Solly's going to grow up and build God a temple.

NARRATOR: So, when David became old, he named Solomon king of Israel.

ACT I, Scene II
Cast:
Narrator
The Lord

Solomon
Bailiff
Women 1 and 2

SOUND EFFECTS Play organ music or light jazz in background. Announcer says: ("Once, as young Solly was up late wrestling with the affairs of state, he fell asleep and had a dream . . .")

THE LORD: Psst! Solomon, wake up!
SOLOMON: Hmmm. Oh. *(yawning)* Wha'. . . what? Who are You?
LORD: I'm the Lord. Don't you recognize Me?
SOLOMON: Huh? Oh! Yes, Lord, sorry, I must have dozed off. I didn't hear You come in. *(rubbing eyes)* What do You want?
LORD: I want to make you an offer.
SOLOMON: What kind of an offer, Lord? What do You want me to do for You?
LORD: I want to do something for *you* since your father was such a good friend. What do you want? I'll give you anything you want: wealth, long life, fame, death for your enemies. You name it, it's yours.
SOLOMON: Anything?
LORD: I said anything, didn't I?
SOLOMON: Um, can I think about it?
LORD: Sure, I've got all the time in the world. But you don't. Let's make it five seconds.

SOUND EFFECTS: Clock ticks five times.

LORD: Your time's up.
SOLOMON: Oh, don't say that. It sounds so, so, final.
LORD: Sorry. Well, what have you decided? Wealth? Fame?
SOLOMON: Well, actually no. Those things would be great, but what I really need is something to make the king business a little easier. I'm just a kid and I still can't even tell a peasant uprising from a major enemy attack. I don't know how my father did it.
LORD: He had good help.
SOLOMON: What I need is brains.
LORD: You mean wisdom?

SOLOMON: Yes, wisdom.

LORD: Good choice, Solomon. You're sounding more like your dad every day. And since you've chosen something to help others and not just yourself, I'm going to throw in the other things as well. You are going to be the wisest, most famous, wealthiest king of your time.

SOUND EFFECTS: Music fades.

SOLOMON: Wow, thanks Lord! Lord? Where did He go? I must have been dreaming, but what a dream!

NARRATOR: So Solomon became a great ruler. He was fair with his subjects, he discerned right from wrong, and he never ate between meals. Royalty came from all over Asia and Africa to hear him. Of course, he also had to hear a lot of cases involving his subjects. . . .

(Enter Bailiff with two women.)

BAILIFF: The case number 2,357,448 will now be heard before the king. Step forward.

WOMAN 1: Oh, that's us *(bows before Solomon).* Your Highness, this woman here *(Woman 2 comes forward but doesn't bow)* stole my baby. We both live in the same apartment building and had babies at the same time. Her baby died because she rolled over on it in the night! So she switched her dead child with my live one while I was sleeping.

WOMAN 2: That's a lie! Her baby died, not mine.

SOLOMON: No witnesses, huh?

WOMEN 1 AND 2: No, 'fraid not *(glaring at each other).*

SOLOMON: Bailiff! *(Bailiff brings out baby.)* You can halve the baby.

WOMAN 2: That's not fair, giving the child to a third party.

SOLOMON: No, no, no. I asked him to halve the baby—H-A-L-V-E. Cut it in half and give half to each of you. That's fair. Go ahead, Bailiff.

SOUND EFFECTS: Play suspense music.

(Bailiff raises sword over child.)

WOMAN 2: Go ahead. Divide the child. It's fair.

WOMAN 1: No, no. Give the baby to her! Just don't kill it!

SOLOMON *(stands)*: Stop! Give the child to the first woman. She has shown by her love for the baby that it must be hers.

ACT 1, Scene III

Cast:

Narrator

Solomon

Wives 1, 2, and 3

Preacher

Page (messenger)

SOUND EFFECTS Theme Music and Announcer:

("Yes, Solomon was great in the eyes of God and men. He did, however, have one major flaw. He loved some things too much—like weddings.)

(Three wives stand at different places on the stage. Enter Solomon.)

SOLOMON *(turning to first wife)*: Why, you're the only one I've ever loved.

WIFE 1: Ooohh!

SOUND EFFECTS: Church bells ring.

NARRATOR: But, suddenly, Solomon remembers another wedding he must attend on the other side of town.

(Solomon rushes to other side of stage where Wife 2 waits.)

SOLOMON: Um, I do . . . *(looks at Wife 2)* I will at least. *(looks at watch)* Uh, see you later! *(runs to third wife)* I do!

NARRATOR: King Solomon married 700 wives and had 300 concubines. If marrying all these women was a bad idea, he soon had a worse one—he became far less choosy!

(Preacher stands with Solomon and Wife 3.)

PREACHER: And do you both have faith in the Lord Jehovah?

SOLOMON: Oh, yes.

WIFE 3: Jehovah who? I worship this can of peas here.

SOLOMON: Well, they are nice peas. *(Preacher frowns; Solomon shrugs.)*

(Exit, all but Narrator.)

NARRATOR: At that time, even with his busy schedule, King Solomon took time out each week to share his wisdom with the people. Every Thursday at three o'clock the people would gather in the city square to hear the wisdom of Solomon proclaimed.

SOUND EFFECTS: Play trumpet.

(Enter Page.)

PAGE: Thus says King Solomon, as words given from the Lord God Jehovah: "Glad tidings shouted early in the morning are counted as a curse."

NARRATOR: Soon, however, his wives were so many and their gods so varied, he found it necessary to keep a directory in order not to mix up Sybil and her golden eagle with Gloria and her can of peas. Studying this directory took many hours each day, but Solomon still made time to proclaim his wisdom.

SOUND EFFECTS: Play trumpet (muted).

PAGE: Thus says King Solomon: "God helps those who help themselves."

NARRATOR: Sadly, as Solomon spent more time remembering the gods of his many wives, he spent less time remembering the God of his father, David. And so his wisdom became less and less godly. . . .

SOUND EFFECTS: Play trumpet (more muted).

PAGE: Thus says Solomon: "Today is the first day of the rest of your life."

NARRATOR: . . . and now the people were less and less impressed.

SOUND EFFECTS: Play trumpet (very muted).

PAGE: Did you hear the latest from Solomon? "Never wear plaid pants with a striped shirt."

NARRATOR: Nevertheless, Jehovah remained faithful to Israel because of His love for Solomon's father, David. Solomon enjoyed riches and renown like the world had never known; and Jehovah gave Solomon a peaceful reign. All because David had a heart for God. But because Solomon strayed from God, his son, Rehoboam, was not so lucky.

ACT I, Scene IV
Cast:
Narrator
Secretary
King Rehoboam
Punks 1, 2, and 3
Elders 1 and 2

SOUND EFFECTS Theme Music and Announcer: ("One day, soon after Solomon's death, Rehoboam was meeting with his advisers.") (Rehoboam sits at table with elder advisers on one side and punkish peers on the other. Secretary enters.)

SECRETARY: Royal Highness, representatives of the people have assembled in the lobby. They would like their voice heard.

REHOBOAM: And what do they have to say?

SECRETARY: Your father, Solomon, put a heavy tax burden on them. If you will cut taxes and work hours,

they will follow you faithfully. If you don't, well—they won't.

REHOBOAM: Tell them I'll think about it.

SECRETARY: They'd like an answer soon, Sire.

REHOBOAM: All right. Tell them I'll be out in three days to discuss this matter with them.

SECRETARY: Good enough, Sire. *(exits)*

REHOBOAM: Well, Gentlemen, what should I do? *(looks at elders)* You were my father's closest advisers and you've *(looks at punkish peers)* been my best friends since grade school.

PUNK 1: Age before beauty. *(snickers)*

ELDER 1: We think you should comply. Your father built a mighty empire, but you needn't build it anymore. Only maintain it. A happy people is a strong people.

PUNK 2: Whoa! Buckle under? No way. You gotta show 'em who's boss. Tell them your little finger is thicker than your father's leg. If they don't understand that, tell 'em you're doubling the sales tax, income tax, property tax, and then taxing the taxes.

ELDER 2: We think that unwise, Master.

PUNK 3: What are you afraid of, Ray?

(Punks and Elders lean toward center.)

SOUND EFFECTS: Suspense music, ticking.

SECRETARY *(enters)*: Sire, your three days are up.

REHOBOAM: Oh, all right. Gentlemen, I'll be right back.

(Rehoboam exits. Advisers confer with each other.)

REHOBOAM *(returning)*: Well, I did just what you said. I said the thing about my little finger and all that. I told them what a mean, macho king I'd be.

PUNK 3: Right on, King. What did they say? Did they quake and bow and grovel and all that?

REHOBOAM: Um, no. . . they said they're going to go start their own country.

PUNK 1 *(tauntingly)*: That

was bright!

PUNK 2: Good job!

PUNK 3: Oh, way to go, Kingsley.

NARRATOR: And so Israel has remained separated from the House of David from that time until the present day.

ACT II, Scene I
Cast:
Narrator
Elijah, the prophet
Simone (sportscaster)
Derek (sportscaster)
Messenger

SOUND EFFECTS Theme Music and Announcer:
("We return again to 'All My Kings,' the continuing saga of God's dealings with the dynasty of David and the rebel house of Israel.)

NARRATOR: So, after Israel split off from Judah, she turned further and further from the God of David. Again and again the kings of Israel took bad advice. The prophets of false gods told the kings and the people not the truth, but what they wanted to hear. One day, God's prophet, Elijah,

51

decided to take his case to the prophets themselves. He walked right into their hangout and said—

(enter Elijah)

ELIJAH *(to the audience)*: You prophets of Baal and of Asherah just sit around and eat. King Ahab lets you have an easy life here in Israel. But I'm here to tell you that your gods are nothing. Not only can they not predict the future, but your gods can't even cook!

(exit)

NARRATOR: Needless to say, this outraged the prophets of Baal and Asherah. They accepted this as a challenge from Elijah and Jehovah. They agreed to rent the municipal football stadium and invite the people to decide for themselves. Thus began the First Annual Whose God Is Greatest Cook-Off.

SOUND EFFECTS: Loud pep band and crowd.

(Derek and Simone sit on one side of stage.)

DEREK: Here we are, ladies and gentlemen, at the First Annual Whose God Is Greatest Cook-Off. I'm Derek Dindale, your play-by-play announcer for this exciting event, and with me here in the booth is Simone Simmons.

SIMONE: We've got a capacity crowd for this historic event here at Mountainside Stadium.

DEREK: Let's just review the rules for our viewers, Simone. The contest is basically to see whose God can barbecue the best ribs, but there is one catch, isn't there?

SIMONE: Yes, you're right there, Derek. Neither side is allowed to light the fire. That is the job of each respective god. No matches, no lighter fluid, no nothing.

DEREK: And we might also point out to those who just tuned in that the numbers are heavily in favor of the prophets of Baal. See, they have an enormous bench strength—450 first- and second-string prophets.

The challenger, Elijah—a prophet of Jehovah—is aided only by two water boys.

SOUND EFFECTS: A rowdy pep band.

SIMONE: Hey, is it halftime already?

DEREK: No, Simone. The prophets of Baal are taking the field. They've been huddled for quite some time. Now they are moving to carry out their plan.

SIMONE: They sure do look like a marching band to me, Derek. They're spelling "BELP."

DEREK: I think that's supposed to be "HELP." A couple of the second stringers seem to have gotten out of line.

SIMONE: See that, Derek, some of those prophets seem to have hurt themselves, but their god doesn't seem to be responding.

DEREK: My word. You're right. They're . . . They're cutting themselves with knives. There's blood all over the field! This is a terrible day in sports history!

SIMONE: I see Elijah yelling something at the prophets!

ELIJAH *(offstage)*: Hey, you prophets of Baal. You'd better yell louder. Your god can't hear you. Maybe he's just stepped out for a sandwich. Or maybe he's taking a nap. Where is your Baal? You've cut yourselves and he's not watching! What a shame.

DEREK: Well, you heard it. Elijah's having his fun. but his turn is coming—

SOUND EFFECTS: Loud gunshot.

DEREK: Okay, that gunshot indicates the end of the first half. It's been a grueling contest. Now it will be Elijah's chance to show how great his god is.

SIMONE: He's going to hear quite a bit of heckling from the sidelines, to be sure. Those prophets of Baal are not too pleased.

DEREK: Elijah is taking the field with his two assistants now. This is strange; they're digging a trench around the altar. And, huh! They are both carrying buckets of water, probably for a ceremonial washing or something. Elijah couldn't have worked up that much of a thirst already. What—oh, wait a minute! One of the assistants seems to have spilled the water onto the grill.

SIMONE: What a bad break for Elijah. There's no way his god will be able to light that grill now. What's this? The other water boy is doing the same thing!

DEREK: It doesn't look accidental to me, Simone. Look, they're going back for more.

SIMONE: And it seems as if Elijah has instructed them to do this. They soaked down the bullock, the straw, everything! In all my years of announcing, I've never seen anything like it!

DEREK: It certainly doesn't look good for Elijah. His grill is soaking wet. There's water spilling over from the trench and he's just kneeling there in the center of the field. Poor guy.

ELIJAH (*enters and then kneels*): O Lord, God of Abraham, Isaac, and Israel, let it be known today that *You* are the God in Israel and that I'm Your servant. Answer me so that these people will know that You are greatest! You are God.

SOUND EFFECTS: Fans cry out. A very loud crack of thunder.

DEREK: Watch out!
SIMONE: Fire!
DEREK: He's won! Elijah has won!
SIMONE: Jehovah is the greatest!
DEREK: What an exciting moment. That grill just burst into flames, barbecuing the ribs, the wood, the water, everything!
SIMONE: Incredible. It's unbelievable.
DEREK: The whole crowd is chanting, "Jehovah is great! Jehovah is God!"
SIMONE: Right they are, Derek. He's proven that today.
DEREK: Look at the people. They're chasing the prophets of Baal. Looks like they're pretty angry at being duped all these years

about who is really God!

SIMONE: Right you are, Derek. I wouldn't want to be in their sandals today! *(Exit Simone and Derek. Enter Elijah and Messenger.)*

NARRATOR: And so Elijah made an impression on the people. Not too long after that, to Elijah's door came a messenger.

SOUND EFFECTS: Suspense music.
(The messenger hands Elijah telegram.)

ELIJAH: It's from the palace! Could it be a medal? Or maybe a trophy? Or a simple "thank-you" for making clear whose God is great? I guess I'll open it. Oh, it's from Queen Jezebel, wife of King Ahab. Let's see . . . *(Reads telegram.)* "You have seen to it that my friends, the prophets of Baal, have been killed. Now the same will be done to you by noon tomorrow."

SOUND EFFECTS: Dum de dum dum.
NARRATOR: Elijah had 24 short hours to decide. Should he seek to escape or should he confront the queen? Should he apologize or should he try to get rid of her, too? Twenty-four short hours. The minutes ticked off.

SOUND EFFECTS: Tick, tick, tick.

ACT II, Scene II
Cast:
Narrator
King Hezekiah
Nurse
Isaiah, the Prophet

SOUND EFFECTS Theme Music and Announcer:

("Elijah ran from the wrath of Jezebel. Eventually, the Lord got rid of her and Elijah went on to do many incredible things before his time was up. And the Lord continued to send prophets to help His chosen people. One of them was Isaiah. He helped Hezekiah, one of Judah's greatest kings.")

(Hezekiah is lying on hospital bed. Nurse enters.)

NURSE: How are you feeling this morning, King

Hezekiah?

HEZEKIAH: Oooooh!

NURSE: That's just fine. I'm Nurse Mizpah and I just have a few questions I have to ask you.

HEZEKIAH: Ooooh!

NURSE: Have you written your will yet?

SOUND EFFECTS: Suspense music.

HEZEKIAH: My will? Hey, what are you trying to tell me? This is more than just a flu, isn't it? I'm going to die, aren't I, Nurse?

NURSE: Now, please don't breathe in my direction, King.

HEZEKIAH: Don't you hold anything back.

NURSE: Well, I hate to make things sound bad, but—well here, listen to your heart. *(Nurse hands Hezekiah stethoscope, which he uses.)*

SOUND EFFECTS: Heartbeat, that is thumping wildly and erratically.

HEZEKIAH: This is terrible.

NURSE: No, it's a pretty good stethoscope, actually.

HEZEKIAH: I mean my heartbeat. Isn't there something that can be done for me?

NURSE: Not really. You've got the worst boils I've ever seen.

HEZEKIAH: Can't I get a second opinion?

NURSE: Sure. I think your dandruff is disgusting, too!

HEZEKIAH: Be serious.

NURSE: Well, I'm afraid there's . . . .

SOUND EFFECTS: Suspense music.

NURSE: No hope.

(Enter Dr. Isaiah.)

ISAIAH: Wait, Nurse, I've just received a prescription from the Lord our God Jehovah.

HEZEKIAH: Thank you, Isaiah, you're always there when I need you!

ISAIAH: Don't thank me— thank God. He has heard your plea and has granted you 15 more years.

HEZEKIAH: That's wonderful. What is the prescription? Some kind of chemotherapy?

ISAIAH: No.

HEZEKIAH: One of those special diets?

ISAIAH: No.

HEZEKIAH: Antibiotics?

ISAIAH: No.

HEZEKIAH: I know, it's positive mental attitude!

ISAIAH: No, it's figs.

HEZEKIAH: Figs? Oh, Doc, I'd rather die!

ISAIAH: No, Hez, you don't have to eat them. We're going to put them on your boils. You'll live longer, but you might have a problem with fruit flies for a while.

ACT II, Scene III
Cast:
Narrator
Proclaimer
Ezra, the Priest
Boys
People
Nehemiah, the Prophet

SOUND EFFECTS: Theme Music and Announcer:

(After Hezekiah's reign, things again went downhill. The kings that followed—Manasseh and Amon—rejected God and His prophets. It wasn't until Hezekiah's great-grandson, Josiah, took the throne that things began to improve. He had a tough job ahead of him.")

(Josiah sits on one side of stage; Assistant stands next to him.)

ASSISTANT: We have a report here, Your Highness, on the remodeling of the Temple.

JOSIAH: Good. I really want to fix up the Lord's House.

ASSISTANT: The Lord's House, yeah. Well, look, King. One thing we have planned is to change the name.

JOSIAH: The name?

ASSISTANT: Oh, yes. To something which is more accurate—The Community Inspiration and Health Center.

JOSIAH: The Community—

ASSISTANT: Sure. Besides fixing the walls, the builders are installing a game room, and an olympic-size swimming pool, and also weight equipment.

JOSIAH: But what about God?

ASSISTANT: O Your Highness, you insult me to think

I have forgotten about the gods—

JOSIAH: Gods?

(Hilkiah and Workers enter on other side of stage.)

ASSISTANT: Let me show you the commercial we made for television.

SOUND EFFECTS: Commercial jingle.

HILKIAH *(moving downstage with the Assistant)*: Howdy, this here's Hilkiah, the high priest, with an important message about the all-new Community Inspiration and Health Center. That's right, Friends, I said, "Community Health Center." Yes, now the Lord's House can be your house as well. After the construction is finished, you will be able to enjoy—for a small membership fee—the finest in sports and health facilities. And that's not all. . . .

(Workers find a book and examine it.)

ASSISTANT: The new center will also feature a video game room, a McFigburger restaurant, and lots of free parking. But, you say, what about worship? Are there worship facilities? Well, friends, we have developed the most advanced worship processes from Dan to Beersheba. We have a fine chapel where you can worship the god of your choice.

HILKIAH: That's correct, we've got eight gods and no waiting. And come in and try our drive-through altar, where you can get that burnt offering out of the way early and have the rest of the day to yourself. And we've also got . . . . *(Workers hand him a book; one whispers in his ear.)* We've also got the, er . . . *(Hilkiah looks at book.)* the Book of the Law. Book of the Law? Heh, heh? So come on down. See you then. *(Hilkiah brings book to Assistant.)* Look what I've found—the Book of the Law!

ASSISTANT: Nonsense! *(takes book)* There hasn't been a copy of that around here in years.

HILKIAH: Some laborers found it in one of the holes

in the Temple wall.

JOSIAH: What is this book?

ASSISTANT: It is a copy of the agreement God made with Moses and Israel on Mount Sinai.

JOSIAH: I'd love to hear it. Read it to me.

ASSISTANT: It's rather too long, Sire.

JOSIAH: Read it!

ASSISTANT (opens book and reads): "I am the Lord your God, who brought you out of Egypt, out of slavery. You shall not have any other gods before me. You shall not make for yourself an idol—"

JOSIAH: No idols? We've got them all over. I think we are in big trouble. Our nation has been doing just what we weren't supposed to do.

HULDAH (entering): Your Highness, I'm sorry to barge in, but I have some important news for you.

ASSISTANT: Oh, Huldah. I've been meaning to ask your father-in-law, the wardrobe keeper, what ties are doing this year.

HULDAH: They're going wider. And double-breasted tunics are in, too. You want to place an order?

JOSIAH: Hey, wait. Don't you have a message from the Lord? You are a prophetess, aren't you?

HULDAH: Oh, yes, sorry. It's tough wearing two hats, so to speak. Seriously, King, the Lord has heard your trouble and, because you wish to follow Him and fix up the country, the nation will have peace for the rest of your life.

SOUND EFFECTS: Victory bridge music.

HULDAH: However—

SOUND EFFECTS: Defeat bridge music (same band as previous sound effects).

HULDAH: Destruction will come to Judah for its wickedness after your death.

JOSIAH: Well, I'd better not take any chances. We have to get rid of those idols and give the Temple back to God.

(Josiah whispers to Hilkiah, who nods and moves to the other side of stage as Narrator speaks.)

NARRATOR: Then Josiah burned all the idols, reinstituted the holy feasts to honor God, and issued new commercials describing the Temple.

HILKIAH: Come on down, folks, to the Temple. That's right, it's just the Temple again. We don't have any games or swimming pools, but we do have the one true God. See you this Sabbath!

ACT III, Scene I
Cast:
Narrator
Zedekiah, the King
Hananiah, the False Prophet
Jeremiah, the Prophet

SOUND EFFECTS Theme music and Announcer:

("Yes, it's time again for 'All My Kings,' the continuing saga of the Jewish nation as it drifts further and further from the Lord God.")

NARRATOR: The reforms of Josiah lasted for a time, but soon the people went back to false gods and false prophets. They burned incense for gods which were no more than statues of rats, crocodiles, and cartoon characters. All the things God told them to do so they could be happy, they forgot to do. The Lord tried to warn them of their dangers through His two prophets, Isaiah and Jeremiah, but since the people would not accept God's help, the nations of Israel and Judah were destroyed by other countries. Israel fell first and its people were carried off to Assyria. The Lord allowed Judah to exist longer than Israel for the sake of David, the father of its many kings. Eventually though, Judah, too, fell because of its wickedness.

(Zedekiah, Hananiah are sitting onstage. Jeremiah enters.)

HANANIAH: Don't look up now, but here comes that weirdo, glum Jeremiah. *(snickers)*

ZEDEKIAH: Oh, no. Not the weeping prophet. That guy is so depressing. Doom and gloom, gloom and doom. That's all I ever hear from him.

HANANIAH: What's he got around his neck? Looks like a yoke for oxen. I don't believe it. Hey, Jer! You know you got a yoke around your neck?

JEREMIAH: What?

HANANIAH: I said that, "You've got a yoke around your neck."

JEREMIAH: The yoke's on you, Hananiah, for all the lies you've been prophesying. O King, this is what the Lord Almighty says, "I made the world and everything in it, and I can give it to anyone I please. Now it's Nebuchadnezzar's turn. All nations will serve him until his time is up. If you serve him and bow under his yoke, you'll live, but if you don't, you'll die. So don't listen to these lying prophets who tell you everything is A-OK. It's not.

HANANIAH: Don't listen to this crackpot, King. He's so weird. Yokes aren't in at all this year. Besides, the Lord told me that the Babylonians are going to bring back the stuff they took from the Temple the last time they were here. So don't worry.

ZEDEKIAH: Thanks, Han. You're so comforting. Jeremiah, how can you keep a straight face with that thing around your neck?

JEREMIAH (*looking hurt, shifts yoke*): Sorry. Look, I wish the Babylonians *would* return the golden articles, but I'm afraid there's just no way. Not only will they not return the stuff they stole, they're coming back and they're going to take the rest of the stuff, too—furniture, people, and all. They're going to take it all to Babylon, and that's where it's going to stay until the Lord Himself brings it back.

SOUND EFFECTS: Suspense music.

HANANIAH: I tell you, Zed. Don't listen to this guy. Why, I have it on good authority that within two years this whole Babylonian nonsense will blow over. God's going to remove their yoke from our necks. We're His chosen people, right?

ZEDEKIAH: That's right, we are. Why should I worry? Anyway, Jeremiah, didn't your mother ever tell you if you can't say something nice to someone, don't say anything at all?

JEREMIAH: Hey, I'm not the only prophet who ever preached bad news. Check the record. It's our job to warn people about wars, disasters, plagues, and stuff. Why should you be special? But watch out. Because the only test of the prophet who preaches, "peace, peace," is if his prediction comes true.

HANANIAH: Why you!

SOUND EFFECTS: Crack!

HANANIAH: Just like I broke your stupid yoke, the Lord is going to break our yoke. I'm telling you. Two years and it'll all be over.

JEREMIAH: Han, you just made a big mistake. You've broken a wooden yoke: in its place you'll get a yoke of iron. Hananiah, the Lord has not sent you, but you've deceived these peo-

ple into thinking everything is all right. This is what the Lord says, "Your days are numbered. I'm going to remove you from the face of the earth."

SOUND EFFECTS: Suspense music.

NARRATOR: Sure enough, two months later, Hananiah was dead, and the prophecies of Jeremiah came true. Jerusalem was destroyed, the Temple was ransacked, and all the people were carried off to exile into Babylon where they stayed until the Lord raised up the Persians to give Babylon a taste of its own medicine.

ACT III, Scene II
Cast:
Narrator
Belshazzar, Babylon's King
Wives 1, 2
Nobles 1, 2
Steward
Astrologer
Magicians 1, 2
Daniel
Queen

SOUND EFFECTS Theme mu-

sic and Announcer:

("*For almost seventy years God's people lived in exile in Babylon. At last, a new king came to power who knew nothing about the people of Judah. But many of God's people had been faithful to Him in exile and cried out for rescue. One of the most famous was Daniel.*")

SOUND EFFECTS: *Crowd sounds and clinking glasses.*

(*Belshazzar, Nobles, and Wives onstage.*)

BELSHAZZAR: Having a good time, Dear?

WIFE 1: Great party, Bel, but I don't think we have enough glasses.

BELSHAZZAR: You are right. This party seems to have grown. Are those friends of yours over there?

WIFE 1: My friends? No, I thought they were your relatives. They look just like you in those lampshades.

BELSHAZZAR: Steward!

STEWARD (*entering*): Yes, Your Highness?

BELSHAZZAR: We seem to be rather short of cups.

STEWARD: I'm afraid, Sire, that all the royal goblets are in use.

BELSHAZZAR: Can we use the everyday stuff?

STEWARD: We are. All of that's gone, too.

NOBLE 1: Hey, I know what we can use. Remember those great gold and silver goblets your father took from that temple in Jerusalem? Nobody's ever used those.

WIFE 2: Ooh, I remember those pretty things. Let's use those.

NOBLE 2: Yes, why not? They're just gathering dust in the storehouse.

BELSHAZZAR: You heard the people, Steward. Bring on the sacred goblets! More wine all around!

(*Steward exits, returns with goblets.*)

WIFE 2: See, I told you they were pretty.

WIFE 1: Yes, and the wine even tastes better in these. Let's drink a toast to the gods of gold and silver!

NOBLE 1: Ahem. Hear, O hear! Praise be to the gods

63

of gold and silver!

NOBLE 2: Praise to the gods of bronze!

WIFE 2: Don't forget iron. Praise to the gods of iron.

NOBLE 1: And wood!

NOBLE 2: And stone!

BELSHAZZAR: Ha, ha, ha! You guys are a riot! Praith the godth of thone and . . . Huh? What's that?

SOUND EFFECTS: Suspense music.

WIFE 1: The king! He's fainted! What did he see?

WIFE 2: Over there, on the wall. Who wrote that graffiti?

NOBLE 1: Never mind who wrote it. What does it say? *(pause)* Oh, the king's coming to.

BELSHAZZAR *(moaning and dazed)*: A hand. I saw a hand.

NOBLE 2: Somebody give him a hand.

(All clap.)

BELSHAZZAR: Thank you. No. I mean I saw a hand writing on the wall.

WIFE 2: Who was it? Some punk? I know it wasn't one of my kids.

WIFE 1: Are you trying to say one of my kids did it? Why, you . . .

BELSHAZZAR: Ladies, ladies. It wasn't a kid. It wasn't anybody. It wasn't even attached to an arm!

SOUND EFFECTS: Suspense music.

NOBLE 1: A message from the gods?

NOBLE 2: What does it say?

BELSHAZZAR: I, I don't know, but I intend to find out. Steward! Bring in the astrologer and magicians. A third of my kingdom to the one who can tell me this riddle.

(Steward exits, returns with astrologer and magicians.)

ASTROLOGER: Uh, uh, according to my charts, Mars is in conjunction with the man on the moon, and so . . .

BELSHAZZAR: You idiot! Get him out of here. Off with his head!

MAGICIAN 1: Watch this, sire. Pick a card, any card.

MAGICIAN 2: I'll make it

disappear. Abracadabra, ah good and . . . oops.

BELSHAZZAR: Off with their heads, too! Numbskulls! Isn't there a soothsayer worth his salt in all my kingdom?

(Enter the Queen.)

QUEEN: O King, live forever. Even if you didn't invite me to your party. I hear what's going on here. You ought to get Daniel, that Hebrew your dad brought from Jerusalem. He used to be a pretty important guy around here. Could interpret dreams, bring messages from the Lord God, and everything.

BELSHAZZAR: Oh, yeah. I remember him. Strange guy. Vegetarian, wasn't he? Steward! Bring me Daniel, the Hebrew.

NARRATOR: And so Daniel was brought before the king and interpreted the message that God had sent to wicked King Belshazzar.

DANIEL: Mene, mene, Tekel, Parsin. Oh, no.

SOUND EFFECTS: Suspense music.

DANIEL: You really want to hear this, King?

BELSHAZZAR: I don't care how bad it is. I've got to know. Tell me.

DANIEL: OK. You asked for it. *Mene* means your days are numbered. Your reign is over. *Tekel.* That means, on a scale of 100, you come out about zero—roughly translated. And *Parsin* means you're about to lose it all to the Medes and the Persians.

SOUND EFFECTS: Suspense music.

NARRATOR: That's exactly what happened. That very night, Babylon was captured and destroyed by the Medes, and Belshazzar was killed.

ACT III, Scene III
Cast:
Narrator
Proclaimer
Ezra, the Priest
Boys
People
Nehemiah, the Prophet

SOUND EFFECTS Theme music and Announcer:

("Things still looked bad for the Hebrews, but, even in a foreign land, Jehovah did not abandon His people—and He sent prophets in those dark years to remind them of just that. One day, a proclamation was made.")
SOUND EFFECTS: Trumpet.

(Enter Proclaimer.)

PROCLAIMER: Thus says the mighty King Cyrus, king of Persia: "Jehovah, the God of Heaven, has given me all the kingdoms of the earth, but He is the King of kings. He has ordered me to rebuild His Temple in Jerusalem. All those who call Judah home should now return there. There's work to be done."
SOUND EFFECTS: People cheering, trudging.

NARRATOR: Work, yes indeed. Some *twenty* years later, the Temple was completed. There was great rejoicing among the people.

SOUND EFFECTS: Cheers.

NARRATOR: But then time slipped away. . . .

SOUND EFFECTS: Cheers

from previous band fade.

NARRATOR: And so did the people from their God. Sixty years later almost nobody could remember what the Temple was even there for. One day, Ezra, an unemployed priest, took a trip from his home in Babylon to Jerusalem. He was saddened by what he saw.

(Ezra walks up to boys playing handball on back wall of stage.)

EZRA: Excuse me, boys, I'm looking for the Temple of the Lord God Jehovah.
BOY: Huh?
EZRA: The Temple. The building Jehovah presides over. It's a large stone building about that size. *(He points at wall.)* I'm visiting from Babylon and I've been told the Temple is at the corner of Mule Avenue and David's Boulevard.
BOY: That's right here, but there ain't no Temple. This building is gonna be a boys' club or a bowling alley or something fun. I'm hoping they tear it down to make a ball field.

EZRA (excited): But this is the Temple of the Lord! Jehovah lives here.

BOY: Well, He must have moved, 'cause this building has been abandoned for a long time. Nobody lives here now.

NARRATOR: But Ezra had heard enough. With the help of the king of Babylon, Ezra saw to it that the Temple did not become a bowling alley. He began holding services again and taught the people of Judah about the Law of Moses. Things were going well again. In fact, things were going almost too well. . . .

SOUND EFFECTS: Suspense music.

(Ezra shakes hands with People as they leave one side of stage— the Temple. People are saying, "Great sermon, I love the way you preach, is that a new tie, etc." Enter Nehemiah.)

NEHEMIAH: You get a lot of visitors here, don't you?

EZRA: Oh, yes. The people come from all around. It's wonderful too. We're so accessible.

NEHEMIAH: Yes, I noticed that the walls around Jerusalem are still demolished and the gates have been burned. It looks rather disgraceful to me. Why, your enemies, the Samaritans, can come and go in the city as they please. There isn't much to keep them from running you all out of Jerusalem if they wanted.

EZRA: Well, I'm afraid we can't keep them out.

NEHEMIAH: Not without a wall, anyway.

EZRA: What can we do?

NEHEMIAH: Well, I have quite a bit of influence with the king. You see, I'm here visiting.

EZRA: Did you fill out a visitor's card?

NEHEMIAH: Yes, I did; but my home is in Babylon.

EZRA: You're from Babylon? So am I! Do you know. . . . (Ezra and Nehemiah walk off talking.)

EPILOGUE
Cast:
Narrator
Malachi, the Prophet
Listeners 1, 2, 3

NARRATOR: Ezra and Nehemiah had lunch together that afternoon; and so began their partnership—you might even say a match made in Heaven. Nehemiah rebuilt the walls and Ezra continued to rebuild the people, teaching them the Scriptures and speaking out for God. Their work together peaked with a week-long seminar of Scripture teaching by Ezra and his crusade staff. The Scriptures were explained from morning 'til night. A revival broke out as a result of guest speaker, Malachi, who came with a message from Jehovah in the form of a joke.

(Listeners 1, 2, and 3 sit in audience. Enter Malachi.)

MALACHI: Dear Hebrew friends, I come to you with good news and bad news.

LISTENER 1: What's the good news?

MALACHI: The good news is, the Lord is coming. The Messiah promised by the prophets before me will come after all.

LISTENERS: Yea, o yippee, hooray, etc.

MALACHI: The bad news is the Lord is coming, but He's angry.

LISTENERS: Oooh, uh-oh, yikes!

MALACHI: God is looking for obedience in His people. Instead, He sees a people just sitting around waiting for Him to do something. Well, if you wait much longer, He will do something, but you won't like it.

LISTENER 2: Tell us the good news again. Please?

MALACHI: God says He will not only purify the offerings of His people, He's going to purify the people themselves. Jehovah will once again welcome His people as His own. You will be oppressed no longer, and you will no longer have cause to be afraid of Him, He says.

LISTENER 3: No more oppression? What about our oppressors?

MALACHI: You want justice? It's on the way. It will be like a fire burning up your enemies. But for you the sun of righteousness will shine out with healing in its rays. That great and terrible day is coming when the line of David will once again rule God's people.

LISTENER 1: Is it coming soon?

MALACHI: Oh, you never mind when. You remember the Law of Moses and obey it. When the day of the Lord is upon us, the Lord will send the prophet, Elijah, to prepare the way.

NARRATOR: Malachi was referring to John the Baptist, but then, that is another story.

SOUND EFFECTS Theme Music and Announcer:

("So God's covenant with David would be honored.")

JOB

Adapted by Douglas Olsen

This drama, written for teens and young adults, presents the epic story of the suffering and final triumph of Job. Staging and costuming directions are included with each act.

Cast:
VOICE OF GOD
VOICE OF SATAN
JOB
JOB'S WIFE
FOUR MESSENGERS
ELIPHAZ
BILDAD
ZOPHAR
ELIHU

Scene

The ancient land of Uz. An outdoor altar made of stones. Job, dressed in a bright cloak, kisses his wife, who is beautifully attired. He then begins offering sacrifices.

Prologue

Job 1:1—2:13

JOB: *(looking up in prayer)* O glorious God, my Lord, accept these offerings on behalf of my sons and daughters in case they have sinned in their hearts against Thee. Do forgive them, O Lord, our God. *(He continues offering sacrifices throughout the following dialogue.)*

VOICE OF GOD: Satan, have you noticed my servant Job in your travels across the earth? There is no one on earth as devout as Job is.

VOICE OF SATAN: Oh, I have noticed Job. But would he worship You so faithfully if he weren't so prosperous? Of course, he worships You. But what if everything he has were taken away from him? I bet he would curse You then.

GOD: What? Job? Curse Me? Not Job. In fact, I'll show you. You may take everything away from him. You will see, he'll still bless Me. Only you can't hurt Job himself.

SATAN: It's a deal. I'll have Job an atheist before I'm through.

(Job is still offering sacrifices. A messenger comes running in from off stage and falls breathlessly at the feet of Job.)

MESSENGER 1 *(still out of breath)*: Master, master. I have terrible news. We were plowing when suddenly, the Sabeans attacked us. They stole all your donkeys and cattle and killed all the servants except me. Only I escaped to tell.

(Job is stunned, shakes his head in anguish. A second messenger runs in.)

MESSENGER 2: But that is not all. You won't believe what else has happened. I've never seen anything like it. You won't believe it.

JOB: I won't if you don't get around to telling me.

MESSENGER 2: Sir, lightning has struck all your sheep and all your shepherds. They're all dead. I'm the only one who escaped.

JOB: 7000 sheep? And my shepherds, my servants, my cattle, and my donkeys all gone? All I have left are my camels.

(A third messenger runs in.)

MESSENGER 3: I'm sorry, sir, but your camels, too, are gone. Three bands of Chaldeans attacked. They killed all the other servants and stole all the camels.

JOB: What is happening? How can all this be happening to me?

(A fourth messenger runs in.)

MESSENGER 4: There is more!

JOB: More? How can there be more? No, not my—

MESSENGER 4: It is the most tragic news of all.

JOB (horrified): My family? What happened?

MESSENGER 4: They were feasting at your oldest son's. A storm came up out of the desert. It blew down the house and killed them all. Woe is me, that I have escaped to tell you such terrible news. (Job lets up a loud wail and throws himself on the ground. Then slowly he raises himself to his knees and prays.)

JOB: Lord, I was born with nothing, and I will die with nothing. You give and You take away. Blessed be Your name. (He gets up and offers another sacrifice.)

VOICE OF GOD: Well, Satan, looks like I've won. Job still blesses me and worships me, even though you have taken everything away from him.

VOICE OF SATAN: Yes, so far. But, after all, he still has his health. Suppose now he were to suffer in his body. Then he'd curse You!

72

GOD: You think so? We'll see. Job is again in your power. But you may not kill him.

SATAN: I won't need to.

(Job suddenly cries out in pain. He writhes and scratches his body and moans. He throws off his cloak, revealing ragged clothes. Then weakly he tries to offer a sacrifice.)

JOB'S WIFE (entering in ragged costume): Job, I can't stand it any longer. We've lost everything and now you are plagued with boils and still you offer sacrifices. Why don't you just curse God and die?

JOB (weakly): God gave us many good things, and we welcomed them. How can we complain if now He gives us trouble?

JOB'S WIFE: What kind of God is it, that would give us all this trouble? I don't understand you, Job. (She leaves angrily.)

(Job moans and throws dust on his head.)

(Eliphaz, Bildad, and Zophar enter.)

BILDAD: Let's ask this beggar.

ELIPHAZ: You there. Could you tell us where we might find a man called Job?

ZOPHAR: He's the most important man in this land, but we hear he's fallen on hard times. We've come to comfort him.

JOB: What? Bildad, Eliphaz, Zophar. My friends. I am Job.

(They are all shocked. They wail and moan, and like Job throw dust on their heads.)

First Cycle of Speeches

JOB: O God, why was I ever born? Why didn't You let me die in my mother's womb? I'd be happy now. I'd be resting peacefully in the earth with mighty kings and rulers instead of living in all this misery. Why must I suffer so?

ELIPHAZ: Job, may I say something? Don't you have hope that God will bring you through this trouble because of your good, honest life? When has a righteous man ever been ruined? God must be rebuking you for some evil in your life. If you turn to Him for forgiveness, He will prosper you again.

JOB: The only thing I want from God is death. Nothing comforts me. Look, my body is full of sores and scabs and worms. I can't even sleep at night. *(prays)* O God, leave me alone! Why is man so important to You that You should constantly watch and test him?

BILDAD: Listen to me, Job. If, perhaps, you haven't sinned, then your children have sinned, and God punished them as they deserved. But plead with God, and if you yourself are honest and pure, he will restore everything to you and even more.

JOB: Even though I am innocent, all I can do is beg for mercy from Him—if He would even listen to me. He torments me. He holds me guilty even though I have always obeyed Him. So what can I do? I can't take Him to court. Who would act as a lawyer

73

between us?

ZOPHAR: How I wish God would answer you! You claim you are innocent. I say God is punishing you less than you deserve.

JOB (*sarcastic*): Thank you for your wisdom, all three of you. You are so wise that when you die, wisdom will die with you. What you are saying, everyone already knows. But the fact is that I am righteous and blameless; God used to answer my prayers. Now, however, I have troubles and you, my friends, laugh at me. But my argument is with God, not you. (*prays*) Oh, God, stop punishing me and filling me with fear. Tell me what my sins are. Why are You treating me as if I were Your enemy? I wish I could hide in the world of the dead until Your anger at me was over. All You do is wear me down with pain like water wears down rocks.

Second Cycle of Speeches

ELIPHAZ: God offers you

comfort, but instead you're angry with Him. Let me warn you, Job, proud and rebellious men will wither and never be fruitful again, just like all wicked men.

(*Elihu, a younger man, enters and listens for a while.*)

JOB: The "comfort" you give is only misery.

BILDAD: Just listen, Job, listen. Your bitterness and anger and sarcasm will do you no good. It's a hard and fast rule that the wicked shall suffer, no matter what you say.

JOB: Even if I have done wrong, what do you care? Why plague me with your advice? You think my troubles are punishment for my wickedness. Can't you see God is causing all my misery, not me? I know God lives, and even after my flesh is eaten away by disease I will see Him and know Him, and He will judge you for your attitude toward me.

ZOPHAR: Job, you insult us. I can give you a long list of cases to prove that evil men suffer for their evil.

JOB: And I can give you a long list of cases where evil men have grown old and prospered.

Third Cycle of Speeches

ELIPHAZ: Job, you must have committed many sins yourself. Make peace with God and stop treating Him like an enemy. Throw away all your ill-gotten gold and let Him be your gold. He will rescue you if you are innocent.

JOB: No, I would still complain to God—if I could find Him. But I can't find Him anywhere. I have always done His commands. There are thieves and other evil men who reject God. Let a day be set aside where God may judge us all, and you will see I am not like one of them.

BILDAD: I repeat. All-powerful God punishes evil, and no one can be righteous in His eyes.

JOB: Still I swear by Almighty God Himself, who treats me unjustly and makes me bitter, that I will never say anything evil or tell a lie, and I will insist that I'm innocent until the day I die. If I have done evil things—stolen the land for my farm or made people starve—I will confess it to God.

Elihu's Speech

ELIHU: I have been reluctant to speak so far because I'm young and you're old. But it is God, not age, that gives men wisdom. I listened patiently while you all spoke, and you have not disproved Job's arguments. So let me give my own answer to Job.

Now, all of you listen. Job, you claim that God attacks you for no reason. You think you know why God does things? And you three, Eliphaz, Bildad, and Zophar, you also claim that you have all the answers about God. Let me tell you something. No one has all the answers about God. He is far beyond us.

Job, you claim that God never speaks to you. I say

that God is a great Teacher.

He speaks to us in many ways, but we ignore Him. He speaks in dreams. He also speaks to men through suffering. He sends sickness to correct man's evil ways. Sometimes He sends an angel to remind a man of his duties. You are suffering, Job, because God is teaching you something.

Man needs to repent before God and confess his sins. Look at that storm approaching. That is the work of God.

He makes the rain and thunder and lightning and snow. It's all done at His command. Do you know how He does it? No. His power is so great we cannot come near Him.

(The storm comes with a great rushing of wind. Use sound effects, if possible. Above it is heard the voice of God.)

God's Questions

GOD: Job, who are you to question My wisdom with all your ignorant words? Stand like a man and answer My questions, if you can.

Have you ever commanded a day to dawn? Have you ever been to the bottom of the sea? Do you know where light comes from? Who makes rain fall where no one lives?

Do you feed the lions and the ravens in the wilderness? Do you know the ways of wild deer and goats and donkeys and oxen? Are they in your control? Was it you, by the way, Job, who made horses so strong and fast? And what about eagles? Do they behave at your commands? Job, you challenged Me. Will you give up or answer Me?

JOB: What can I say? I was foolish. I will be quiet.

GOD: Come now, stand like a man and answer My questions. Are you trying to put Me in the wrong? Are you as strong as I am? I created you and I created the hippopotamus whose bones are as strong as bronze. And what about the crocodile? Can you put a rope on him as if he were a pet bird? There is no creature on earth that he fears.

Job Responds to God

JOB: I realize, Lord, that You are almighty. You can do anything You wish. I talked without really understanding. Before, I knew only what others had told me. Now I have experienced You myself. So I am ashamed of my attitude and will now repent in dust and ashes. *(He does so.)*

Epilogue

GOD: Eliphaz, Bildad, and Zophar, I am angry with you because you didn't speak the truth about Me the way My servant Job did. Now take seven bulls and seven rams to Job and offer them as a sacrifice. Job will pray for you , and I will answer his prayer. And Job shall receive twice as much as he had before plus seven more sons and three more daughters. And Job will live to a very great age.

THE NEW PILGRIM'S PROGRESS

Allegorical Drama for Young Teens
by Jack Spiers

This allegorical drama, based on John Bunyan's book, can be performed by older elementary and junior high students.

CHARACTERS:

Christian—a youth in search of the Heavenly City

Evangelist—a man who persuades natives of Destruction to go to the Heavenly City

Goodwill—keeper of the gate

Faithful—a friend of Christian, also going to the Heavenly City

Giant Despair—servant of the Wicked Prince

Peace—the spirit of Christian's deceased mother

Shining One—an angel

Charity—keeper of the gate to the Heavenly City

SCENE I

TIME: *The present.*

SETTING: *A country lane bordered by a picket fence. On the fence gate at far right is the sign, "KNOCK, AND IT SHALL BE OPENED." There is a bench beside the lane. Christian is seated on the bench looking sad. Christian wears a backpack. Evangelist, dressed as a minister and carrying a Bible, enters.*

EVANGELIST: Hello, my friend! May I sit with you for a while?

CHRISTIAN (*sadly*): Sure, if you like. I'm afraid, however, that I will be very poor company. I don't feel very well.

EVANGELIST (*patting Christian on the back*): Sometimes good comes out of times that seem to be only bad. I will tell you something which can change your whole outlook on life.

CHRISTIAN: Please do tell me, sir. I don't know why I'm so miserable, but there must be something better than the life I've lived so far. I'm tired of carrying this heavy load on my back.

EVANGELIST: I have the solution to your problem. I'll tell you where to get rid of that heavy load.

CHRISTIAN: Please go on!

EVANGELIST: Years ago your city was placed under a severe judgment because the people were so wicked. Your city will one day be destroyed by fire.

CHRISTIAN: By fire? What should I do?

EVANGELIST: You should leave this city immediately and go to the Heavenly City. There you will be safe.

CHRISTIAN: What about my friends and my dad? What would they think if I left our city of Destruction for this place you mention? Shouldn't I stay here to help them when the trouble comes?

EVANGELIST: No, the only way you will be able to help them is to leave Destruction. This may give them courage to leave also.

CHRISTIAN: My dad is so busy. I'm afraid he won't take time to think about leaving Destruction. My mother left when I was a baby. I remember someone telling me that she went to another city. Do you suppose she went to the Heavenly City?

EVANGELIST: Oh, yes, she lives in the city to which you must go. Her name is Peace. She wanted so much to live in the King's city, and to see the Prince.

CHRISTIAN (*puzzled*): Who are they?

EVANGELIST: The King and His Son, the Prince, reign in the Heavenly City.

CHRISTIAN: How will I find the way there?

EVANGELIST (*pointing to*

the picket gate at far right): You must go to the narrow gate over there and knock. A man named Goodwill waits to tell you where to go and how to find the way.

(Evangelist exits left. Christian walks slowly toward the gate.)

CHRISTIAN *(reading the sign)*: "Knock, and it shall be opened."

(Christian knocks, but nothing happens. After a few seconds he knocks once more. Goodwill, a pleasant old man in modest attire, opens the gate and steps through.)

GOODWILL: Oh, come in. Come in. Eternal glory you will win.

CHRISTIAN: My name is Christian. I have left the city of Destruction as Evangelist told me to do. He said you would show me the way to Heavenly City.

GOODWILL: Yes, and you have done wisely. This way is narrow and few people find it. First, you must travel to the cross.

CHRISTIAN: What makes the Cross a special place?

GOODWILL: The Cross reminds us of what our wonderful Prince did for us. You see, the King once sent His Son to your city of Destruction. The Prince tried to show your people the way to Heavenly City, but they hated Him. They tried to get rid of Him on a wooden cross. Oh, how He suffered, nailed to that cross! Finally He died.

CHRISTIAN: What a sad story!

GOODWILL: But it ends happily. The wicked people couldn't beat the Prince. He came alive again. He's still helping people reach Heavenly City to live forever with Him and the King.

CHRISTIAN *(turning to show his backpack)*: But I'll never make it to Heavenly City carrying this heavy load. Can the Prince help me get rid of it?

GOODWILL: That is why He died—so you could be free of that heavy load. When you reach the cross, just take off your burden and leave it there. As one of the Prince's loyal subjects, you'll never have to carry that burden again.

CHRISTIAN: What a relief that will be! How do I get to the cross?

GOODWILL: Just take this road. Whenever you come to a fork in the road, choose the way that is more straight and more narrow. Though these roads will seem harder to travel, they alone will get you there.

CHRISTIAN: Thanks. I'll start right away.

(Christian goes through the gate; Goodwill closes it. Both exit.)

SCENE II
TIME: Sunset
SETTING: A meadow with a cross in the center. Christian enters slowly. Seeing the cross, he approaches reverently and kneels, facing the cross. Christian pulls the bow now holding his burden and it falls off. He slowly raises both hands in worship toward the cross. Evangelist enters from left and kneels beside Christian.

EVANGELIST: How wonderful that you have learned the grace of the Cross.

CHRISTIAN (with tearful joy): Yes, I feel so light!

EVANGELIST (very excited): Now you're a child of our King and can go as a pilgrim to His City.

CHRISTIAN: How can I thank you for showing me the way?

EVANGELIST: Showing people the way is my greatest joy.

CHRISTIAN: Please tell my dad and my good friend Faithful what a wonderful thing has happened to me.

EVANGELIST: I will tell your dad but there's no need to tell Faithful.

CHRISTIAN: Why?

EVANGELIST: Because he left Destruction for the Narrow Gate soon after you did.

(Faithful enters burdened and weary. Christian and Evangelist meet him and walk with him to the cross. As he kneels, his burden falls from his back.)

EVANGELIST: By going to live with the King, you have both chosen the greatest treasure possible. Keep it at any cost. The Wicked Prince has many soldiers who work tirelessly at trying to steal this treasure.

EVANGELIST (taking two golden keys from his pocket and giving one to each boy): I give you each a key. If you are ever taken prisoner by the Wicked Prince, your key will allow you to escape. Be careful not to lose it. Now you must go to the Palace Beautiful. There you will learn many useful and precious things. (All exit.)

SCENE III

TIME: The next afternoon.
SETTING: Same country with picket fence border.
Christian and Faithful enter walking wearily.

FAITHFUL: Oh my, these stones are hurting my feet!
CHRISTIAN: Let us climb over the fence and rest on that soft grass for a while.
FAITHFUL: We're not supposed to leave the straight and narrow path. If we step off the path, we'd be on the Wicked Prince's land.

CHRISTIAN: But Faithful, the soft grass is so close to the straight and narrow path of the King. We could get back on the path in a second if we saw anyone coming.

FAITHFUL: All right, but I don't like it (They step over and sink wearily to the ground.)

CHRISTIAN (rubbing his feet): Whew! I'm beat!

FAITHFUL: Yeah, me, too. I think a little nap would help us more than anything. (They lie back on the grass as if to sleep.)

GIANT DESPAIR (enters with chains and a club, speaking in a deep and harsh voice): Who said you could sleep in my meadow?

CHRISTIAN (getting up): We just stepped over the fence to rest a little while. We were so tired of the hard path.

GIANT DESPAIR (threatening them with his club): Nobody walks or sleeps on my land without permission!

FAITHFUL: We will cross back over and never use your meadow again. (He starts to step over.)

GIANT DESPAIR (taking hold of Faithful's shoulder): Not so quick, lad! You must be taught a lesson you won't soon forget. (He wraps a chain around them.)

CHRISTIAN: Please, sir, if you will let us go, we will never set foot on your land again. We are pilgrims of the King!

GIANT DESPAIR (strikes Christian with his club): I hate all pilgrims of the King! I will see to it that you never walk in my meadow again!

(He beats both boys and they fall upon the ground and lie motionless. Giant Despair walks off. Peace enters and tenderly bathes the boys' faces with a white cloth. Christian opens his eyes and recognizes Peace.)

CHRISTIAN: Mother! My dear Mother!

PEACE: Yes, Christian, it's me. I have often been near you in my thoughts. Soon I will be with you forever in the King's city. Good-bye for now. (She slowly and gracefully exits as Christian

watches transfixed.)

CHRISTIAN (thrilled): Faithful, wake up! I saw my mother! She bathed my face and spoke to me!

FAITHFUL (groggily): It, it must have been a dream.

CHRISTIAN: I know I saw her, and that I don't hurt anymore.

FAITHFUL: The King is very good to us. He won't let us suffer more than we are able to bear.

CHRISTIAN: We were to go directly to the Palace Beautiful. It was very wrong of me to suggest leaving the straight and narrow way, though it was rough. How will we get out of these chains? (He suddenly discovers the key in his hand.) Faithful, look! My mother must have taken this key out of my pocket and placed it in my hand.

FAITHFUL: The Key of Promise! Quick, quick, Christian, try to unlock the chains.

CHRISTIAN: I will, and you try your key! (The boys hurriedly unlock their chains and get free of them. Giant

Despair rushes out as the boys cross over the fence and get back on the path.)

GIANT DESPAIR *(beginning to stiffen and fall, as with a seizure)*: Come back! Come back! I hate you and your King! *(He falls as the scene ends.)*

SCENE IV

TIME: *Later that same day.*
SETTING: *The parlor of Charity's home. Charity hears a knock and opens the door to greet Christian and Faithful.*

CHARITY: Come in! You are welcome as long as you need a place to stay. I am Charity.

CHRISTIAN: My name is Christian and this is my friend, Faithful.

CHARITY *(gently)*: Yes, I know. I expected you to get here long before now.

CHRISTIAN *(looking down)*: It's my fault we're late.

CHARITY: I hope that you didn't have any serious trouble.

CHRISTIAN: When we left the way of the King, we were chained and beaten by a giant.

CHARITY: Giant Despair! Oh, you poor boys! Many pilgrims fall into the hands of Despair. He is so harsh and cruel. Well, that is behind you now. You must go on to be better pilgrims.

CHRISTIAN: Yes, it is so easy to make a mistake. But the King was wonderfully kind to help us escape.

CHARITY: There is always a way of escape for the King's pilgrims.

FAITHFUL: We were very foolish to leave the King's path.

CHARITY *(reassuringly)*: But don't be too hard on yourselves. There was only one perfect pilgrim, and that was our dear Prince. Our King always forgives pilgrims for His Son's sake.

CHRISTIAN: I can hardly wait to meet the Prince! *(A knock is heard at the door, and the Shining One enters.)*

SHINING ONE: I have a message that is for you, Christian. It is time for you to enter the City. You must go on alone. You have only one trouble left, and that is crossing the river.

CHRISTIAN: Is it very deep and wide?

SHINING ONE: It appears to be deep and wide at first, but you will find the Prince Himself waiting for you on the other side. When you know He's near, a deep peace and joy will settle over you. You will not be afraid to cross the river.

CHRISTIAN: Faithful, I, I must say good-bye to you. That's hard for me, but I look forward to what is ahead.

FAITHFUL: I will miss you, Christian.

CHRISTIAN: Faithful, I do have one favor to ask of you. Please take a message to my father. Tell him that I will be waiting and watching for him in Heavenly City.

FAITHFUL: Yes, I will take the message. Soon it will be my time to go to the King's city. Then we can be together forever.

(Christian shakes hands with Faithful, then with Charity. The Shining One and Christian exit.)

TRIED AND CONVICTED

A Courtroom Drama
by Jim A. Townsend

This short play, written for older children and teens, depicts the atoning work of Christ through a courtroom battle between Christ and Satan. It might be used in a worship service, retreat, camp meeting, etc.

Cast:
God—the judge
Defendant
Satan—the prosecuting attorney
Jesus—the defense attorney
Jury (made up of as many actors as you want)

COSTUMES AND PROPS: Dress actors in typical courtroom clothing. The judge might wear a black robe and rap a gavel. The prosecuting and defense attorneys might wear suits (Satan could wear horns, and Jesus could have a beard and red splotches on his palms). The stage might look like a courtroom with jury sitting in the choir loft.

GOD *(comes in and sits down; raps gavel)*: We will now hear the case of *(defendant's name)*. Will the defendant approach the judge's bench. *(holds out Bible)*

(Defendant approaches judge's bench and puts hand on Bible.)

GOD: Do you swear to tell the truth, the whole truth, and nothing but the truth, so help you God?

DEFENDANT: I do.

GOD: You may sit down. The accuser will begin his examination of the stated defendant.

SATAN: Judge and jury, today I will prove that the defendant, _____ , is guilty of sin. Thus, he/she deserves to have the maximum penalty. According to Your Law, Your Honor, Romans 6:23 to be exact, the wages of sin is death. *(approach defendant and point a finger at him)* You have broken God's laws. When you were six years old, you disobeyed your mother and didn't come home on time as you had promised. All through school you sometimes told your teachers lies. In church, this church to be exact, you goofed around when you should have been listening.

DEFENDANT: But I did a lot of good things, too.

SATAN: Big deal. According to James 2:10, God's Law, if you sin even once, you are guilty of breaking all God's laws. An "out" is an "out" in baseball, whether you strike out or hit the ball 430 feet into the outfield, where it is caught. Why should you be allowed to live eternally with God? You would pollute Heaven just as you have helped pollute the earth. Now don't try to say you're innocent. In your pocket are red slips of paper on which you have written your confession. You *did* write down some unkind things you did, didn't you?

DEFENDANT: Well . . . yes.

SATAN: Did you hear that, jury? He admits it. He says he's guilty of sin. Even if he didn't admit it, Romans 3:23 says that all people have sinned. The defendant deserves to be separated from God forever. I rest my case. *(He sits down.)*

GOD: Jesus, do You wish to question the witness?

JESUS: Not at this time, Your Honor.

GOD: Jury, we will have a short recess while you reach your verdict.

(God raps gavel. Jury whispers among themselves as if they were discussing the case. Finally they arrive at consensus. One juryman nods to the judge, who raps his gavel.)

GOD: Have you reached your verdict? Members of the jury, you may answer one at a time.

JURY: Guilty. Very guilty. Guilty. Guilty . . .

GOD: According to My Law found in Romans 6:23, all

who sin must die. After death comes My judgment (Heb. 9:27). Be it known, therefore, _____ , I pronounce you guilty as charged. You are sentenced to die, after which time, you will be separated from Me forever.

JESUS *(gets up and goes to bench):* One moment, Your Honor. It is true that the defendant is guilty. But I have already paid the penalty for his sins. As Your Law says in I Peter 3:18, the Just One suffered for the sins of all the unjust ones that they might come to You. I am the Just One, for I never sinned. I died that I might give the defendant My own righteousness. Therefore, My sacrifice should be an acceptable substitute for his death sentence.

SATAN: Wait a minute, Your Honor. *(jumps up)* The defendant is *still* a sinner, and he is guilty. He should suffer forever with me!

GOD: No, not if My Son Jesus claims that the defendant's sins are removed forever. I will accept Jesus' death in place of the defendant's death, that is, if the defendant is one of Jesus' followers. So, tell me: Are you, _____ , one of My Son's disciples?

DEFENDANT: Yes, yes, Your Honor, I am.

GOD: Then, as God and Creator of the Universe, I pardon you. According to My Law as found in Romans 3:24, I give you eternal life with Your Lord, Jesus Christ. Case dismissed.

(He pounds His gavel sharply.)

THE INDESTRUCTIBLE WORD

By Bonnie Ward Elson

This humorous play, adapted from Jeremiah 36, reveals the awesome power of God's Word. It can be performed by older children or teens in 10-15 minutes. It might be part of a worship service, camp meeting, retreat, etc.

Cast:

Narrator
The Voice of the Lord
Jeremiah—God's prophet
Baruch—(Buh-ROOK), Jeremiah's scribe
Micaiah—(my-KAY-uh)
Officials 1, 2, and 3
Jehoiakim—(juh-HOY-uh-kim), king of Judah

Setting:

Judah, about 600 years before Christ was born.

Scene I

NARRATOR: Our story begins after wicked King Jehoiakim has been on the throne of Judah for four years—which is about four years too long in the Lord's opinion. So the Lord speaks to Jeremiah, His prophet. After all, Jeremiah is one of the few people left in Judah who will listen to Him.

THE LORD: Jeremiah, get a scroll, a long scroll. I want you to write all the words I have spoken to you during the past 20 or so years. Perhaps when the people of Judah hear about the disaster I plan to inflict on them, each person will turn from his or her wicked ways; then I will forgive their wickedness and sin.

NARRATOR: So, Jeremiah obeyed God. He called his friend Baruch . . .

JEREMIAH: That's right. I need someone with good handwriting. The person has to be able to write in neat, even columns.

BARUCH: Sure, I'd be glad to take whatever dictation you give. Now what's that bad news you were telling me about?

JEREMIAH: Let me give you a hint. Cancel anything you were going to do in the next year or so . . .

NARRATOR: So Jeremiah dictated all the words the Lord had spoken, while Baruch carefully wrote them on a scroll. About a year later . . .

JEREMIAH: Thus saith the Lord. The end.

BARUCH: We did it! We're finally all done. Let's celebrate!

JEREMIAH: Before you relax, I need another favor.

BARUCH: I don't think I want to hear this.

JEREMIAH: We need to read this scroll to the people. The best place would be the Temple, but I am not allowed to go there.

BARUCH: All of a sudden I know what favor you're going to ask me.

JEREMIAH: Right—I want you to go to the house of the Lord. Read the words of the Lord I dictated. Perhaps the people will turn from their wicked ways, for the wrath of the Lord against them is fierce.

Scene II

NARRATOR: Baruch waited until a day when people had come from far and wide to fast and worship at the Temple. He read the Lord's words from the scroll.

Micaiah, a royal official, heard the doom God was promising for Judah. He ran to the king's secretary's room where all the officials were sitting, trying to keep warm.

MICAIAH: Wait till you hear this! I just heard Baruch read from a scroll at the Temple. He said the Lord is going to destroy our country!

OFFICIAL 1: This I have to hear for myself. Get Baruch to come read that scroll to us.

NARRATOR: Baruch read the scroll to the officials. When he finished, the officials looked at each other in fear.

OFFICIAL 2: The Lord is terribly angry with us! He really is going to destroy our nation if we don't repent.

OFFICIAL 3: We have to report this to the king.

OFFICIAL 1: Right, but who's going to tell him? You will never have seen anger like the king's when he hears this.

OFFICIAL 2: Baruch, you and Jeremiah better hide in a place where nobody can find you. We'll take care of telling this to the king.

Scene III

NARRATOR: While Baruch and Jeremiah found a place to hide, the officials read the scroll to King Jehoia-

kim. The king was sitting in front of a fire to keep warm.

KING JEHOIAKIM (angry): Give me that scroll!

OFFICIAL 3: But your highness, that isn't the whole scroll. I've read only three or four columns!

KING: I said give it to me!

OFFICIAL 2: No, don't cut the scroll, your highness!

OFFICIAL 3: Don't burn the scroll! Those are the words of the Lord!

KING: Silence! Words of the Lord indeed! I'll believe Babylon is going to destroy Judah when I see it.

Servants! Go find those two troublemakers, Jeremiah and Baruch. Arrest them at once!

Scene IV

NARRATOR: No one could find Jeremiah or Baruch because the Lord had helped them hide in a good place. The Lord had seen exactly how much King Jehoiakim and most of the people cared about His words. They had tried to destroy the Lord's words! But you can never destroy the Lord's words, as King Jehoiakim soon found out.

THE LORD: Jeremiah, get another scroll. I want you to write on it everything that was on the first scroll. And here's what I'm going to do to this king and people that ignore My words: King Jehoiakim will have no descendants as king, and he won't even get a decent burial. I will bring on the people every disaster I promised, because they have not listened to My words.

Epilogue

NARRATOR: Our story does not have a happy ending. The people thought they could ignore or destroy God's words rather than obey them, so God did what He promised. The Babylonian army came and crushed Judah without mercy. God's indestructible word came true.